Famous Biographies for Young People

FAMOUS
MODERN CONDUCTORS

FAMOUS MODERN CONDUCTORS

by David Ewen

ILLUSTRATED WITH PHOTOGRAPHS

Dodd, Mead & Company · New York

J
780.922
E

PREFACE

In *Famous Conductors*, published in 1966, this author discussed the careers and achievements of seven of the foremost orchestra and opera-house leaders of the recent past. All these men are now dead. But their influence and their accomplishments are still very much with us.

Famous Modern Conductors continues where the earlier volume left off. A golden dozen are here represented, twelve conductors who dominate the musical scene of our times. All of them were still alive when this book was being written. Some have reached a patriarchal age, while others are comparatively young. Some head major American musical organizations, while others are concentrating their basic activity in Europe. All, however, are conductors of the first importance. All are enriching the musical experiences of concert and opera-house audiences everywhere. And all have made distinguished recordings.

The traditions and techniques which the men in *Famous Conductors* helped to establish in the art and science of conducting are being carried on by the artists written about in *Famous Modern Conductors*. Art, however, does not stand still. A new and greater symphonic and operatic era has been unfolding all around us since the conductors in the earlier volume have lived and worked. And it is the conductors of the present volume who are basically responsible for this continual growth.

64781

CONTENTS

LEOPOLD STOKOWSKI

[Born 1882]

WHEN, AS MUSICAL director of the Philadelphia Orchestra, Leopold Stokowski was in his prime, he was often described as the "Barnum of Music" or as a "prima donna conductor." There was a good deal of truth in both descriptive phrases. Stokowski was a showman second to none. He was blessed with more than the normal quota of temperament allowable to sensitive musicians, and he was an artist who had a gift for attracting publicity.

He flooded the conductor's platform with glamour. His slim, well-proportioned figure was always exquisitely tailored. His bodily gestures had ballet-like grace while the patterns he fashioned in midair with his expressive hands were poetry in motion. He wore his shock of gold hair like a regal crown. All this made him a shining ornament on the dais. Stokowski knew he had visual appeal, and he knew how to heighten and dramatize that appeal.

In Philadelphia it had long been rumored that the Academy of Music stage had been redecorated in vivid silver and blue colors at Stokowski's orders, feeling as Stokowski did that those colors blended best with his flaming blond hair. This may very well be apocryphal. But it is no legend that on one

11

occasion he had a single beam of light shining over his head to create a halo effect; that on another occasion he had the stage lights so adjusted that they could project dancing shadows of his digital movements on the walls and ceiling. When he made his first movie—*The Big Broadcast of 1937*—he instructed the cameras to focus their eyes on those eloquent hands of his.

If Stokowski had a gift for attracting publicity he also had a talent for arousing discussion and controversy. He was always doing the unexpected. At one time he tried to dispense with applause. ("This strange beating of hands has no meaning," he maintained.) At another time he wanted his concerts to take place in a completely darkened auditorium. ("Music," he insisted, "is best heard in darkness.") Innovation and experimentation were the meat and potatoes of his musical diet. Some were interesting, some important, but some were outright quixotic. He was continually introducing novel instruments into the orchestra, such as ether music (Thereminvox), a Hammond tone-sustaining piano, and something called a Clavilux that threw colors on a screen while the music was being played. He was always experimenting with new musical idioms and techniques, by performing quarter and eighth-tone music, twelve-tone music, jazz, oriental music. At one time he eliminated the office of concertmaster, rotating the position so that each of his violinists might get a greater sense of responsibility. He allowed all his violinists to bow freely—that is, each violinist could bow in a way most natural to him instead of conforming rigidly to the movements of all the other violinists in the same upward and downward flight of the bow.

Again and again he would add a footnote or two to conducting history with dramatic "firsts." Long before anybody else did so in the United States he conducted without a score. This was such a novelty in the early 1910s that one of the dowagers in the audience was led to believe that Stokowski did not know how to read music. When a scoreless dais no longer attracted attention, he dispensed with the baton, once again doing something that was unknown at that time in America. He was one of the first conductors to engage women in a major orchestra; and after he left Philadelphia to form other orchestras he was also one of the first to employ Negroes. He was one of the first American conductors to take a major orchestra on a coast-to-coast tour; this was back in 1936. He was the first major conductor in America to make recordings—in 1917 for Victor. Years before the age of hi-fi and stereophonic sound he experimented with ways and means of achieving a more faithful reproduction of orchestral sound. His musical and scientific knowledge helped bring about significant changes and improvements not only in recording music on disks but also in broadcasting it over the radio and fixing it on the soundtrack of a motion picture. For Stokowski was also the first major conductor to present a symphonic program of concert hall standards on an American coast-to-coast program. This happened on October 6, 1929. When he finished that concert he told his unseen audience: "We have been playing good music and that is the only kind we will play. I will not play any popular music. If you do not like this, write and tell us and we will discontinue broadcasting." He was also the first American symphony conductor to appear in the movies. In *The Big Broadcast of 1937* he performed Bach, something that had never before happened in a movie musical and has happened rarely since. In *100 Men and a Girl* he not only conducted but also played a speaking role. After that he collaborated with the Walt Disney studios in producing *Fantasia* in which the music of Beethoven, Stravinsky, Dukas (among others) was married to animated cartoons in

13

little dramatic episodes and ballet sequences.

In short, Stokowski has always been the pioneer who blazed new trails for orchestral music, and on more occasions than one he was responsible for opening new horizons and discovering new worlds.

In Philadelphia he was truly a press agent's delight. Realizing the value of mystery, he kept his origins and backgrounds enshrouded in doubt for a long time. Now he encouraged the belief that he came from Poland, though he had actually been born in England, and he helped support his myth with a thick and not easily definable accent that was some thousand miles east of London. He refused to deny the unfounded rumor that his name was originally less picturesque than Leopold Stokowski—Lionel Stokes to be exact—just as he would neither deny nor confirm the absurd story that circulated in Philadelphia for a while that he was a descendant of Richard Wagner. He even permitted the intriguing air of mystery and doubt to obscure the identity of the man who made those striking orchestral arrangements of Bach's music featured so prominently and frequently on his programs. "Bach is important," he would reply angrily to any inquiry, "not the man who translated him for the orchestra." Eventually, of course, it came out that Stokowski himself was the author of these transcriptions, and in time he even allowed his name to appear hyphenated with that of Bach. But keeping his alter ego in the dark so long undoubtedly helped to keep these Bach pieces a bountiful conversation piece in Philadelphia living rooms for many an evening.

With his volatile moods and contradictory attitudes and behavior he made himself an enigma defying easy solution. This too made for good newspaper copy. He kept the orchestra men at a distance. He never called them by their first names, nor did he allow any exchange of familiar pleasantries. When he passed one of his musicians in the streets he would often fail to recognize him. He could be thoughtless and he could be cruel, without a touch of compassion or feeling humanizing his relationship with his men. Yet time and again he would do favors secretly, now for one musician, now for another; when one of his men had a prolonged, serious illness he was the unidentified benefactor who paid all the hospital bills.

He was not above making a rehearsal or concert the setting for some circus stunt that made front-page news the next day. One day he startled the men by rehearsing while sitting astride a hobby horse. Another day, he burned incense on the stage to set the mood for a piece of oriental music. At one of his concerts he gave the audience an unforgettable object lesson on concert manners. During the performance of the first number he had some of the orchestra players drift in lackadaisically and noisily on their way to their chairs. While the music was played, some of the men started to talk loudly to one another. In the concluding number, some of the men made a rush for the exit even before the music was over. The audience saw the point, laughed, applauded—and continued to be similarly ill-mannered at the next concert.

His weakness for making little impromptu speeches to his audiences was also a good source for newspaper copy. Sometimes he tried to explain and interpret a difficult piece of music. Most often he took the people severely to task. When they responded with frigid silence to the ungodly sounds of some avant garde music he gave them a bitter tongue lashing for their apathy. Then when audiences abandoned apathy to hiss, he excoriated them for their stupidity. On several occasions, when the reaction to some new music was particularly hostile, he would repeat the work—partly with the hope that

15

familiarity would breed tolerance and understanding, partly out of defiance. His other speeches touched on the audiences' habits of chewing gum, coughing, or talking during a performance.

His every foible was fuel to ignite publicity fires. For a long time he was a food faddist, now partial to exclusively heavy meat diets, now subsisting on raw vegetables, nuts, and fruit juices. For a long time he refused to accept any stimulant, however mild, including alcohol, tobacco, and even coffee or tea. He went through a physical fitness phase that involved rigorous setting up exercises each day, and chopping wood. When woodchopping lost its interest for him, he went in for raising flowers, fruits, vegetables, even trees; and he said he loved "watching them grow and preparing the earth for their roots."

His religious preoccupations were also newsworthy. Baptized a Roman Catholic, he became an agnostic. Subsequently he found spiritual guidance and inspiration in various religious beliefs, one at a time—theosophy, Buddhism, the Anglican church, the Quaker cult. He once publicized the fact that much of his inner strength came from hours of silent contemplation, in the manner of an Oriental. In actuality, the one basic religion to which he has remained faithful through the years is derived from nature.

Even his marriages proved to be newsworthy events. His first wife was one of America's leading pianists and music educators, Olga Samaroff. They were married in 1911, before the then unknown Stokowski first came to Philadelphia. It was a stormy union, a clash of artistic temperaments and strong-willed personalities. They parted through divorce in 1923, after Stokowski had become an idol in Philadelphia. His second marriage, in 1926, helped make him a millionaire, his wife being Evangeline Brewster Johnson, the heiress of the giant pharmaceutical house, Johnson and Johnson. They were divorced in 1937. When he married a third time, in 1945, it was once again to an heiress,—Gloria Vanderbilt de Ciccio. He was then sixty-three, she only twenty-one. This marriage, like the other two, was dissolved by divorce—in 1955.

A good case, then, could have been built up for the argument that at the height of his popularity and fame in Philadelphia Stokowski was a publicity seeker who was not above employing questionable tactics to gain attention. But this fact does not obscure another: that he was also a genius whose influence on American music cannot be overestimated. He brought audiences into the concert hall. Half empty when he first took command in Philadelphia, the venerable academy of music soon became overcrowded. These audiences may have come to pay court to a magnetic conductor, but they stayed to hear great symphonic music played superbly. And besides giving wonderful concerts, Stokowski did yeoman service in advancing America's musical intelligence and sophistication and in creating a climate in which modern music—and especially modern American music—could receive sympathetic hearing.

He had inherited a fifth-rate orchestra in Philadelphia, and he transformed it into one of the world's greatest. He weeded out the undesirables, replacing them with young, eminently gifted musicians. He stood ready to pay well for the purchase of virtuosos of the first order for the first-desk positions. With an organizing talent second to none, and an innate gift for welding the separate parts of an orchestra into a single inextricable organism, he created a sensitive instrument which Rachmaninoff once described as "the Stradivarius of orches-

17

tras." Its magical tone—the "Stokowski tone" was the way in which it was often identified—its luscious sonority, its fantastic virtuosity and its army-like discipline made the Philadelphia Orchestra unique.

As a conductor, Stokowski has functioned more with intuition and temperament than with intellectual processes. He has been a dramatist ever conscious of his timing; a poet ever concerned with over-all effect rather than detail. He has reacted to music emotionally rather than analytically, and his best presentations have proved overwhelming emotional experiences. With rare exceptions, he did not first study a score minutely the way other composers might, nor did he put a microscope over each phrase to scrutinize every nuance and effect. He read a score as one might a book, reacting to certain pages more with heart than with mind and skimming over those pages that did not move him. Stokowski never completed his work of preparation and interpretation before coming to rehearsals. He did not even complete his entire job at the rehearsal. At rehearsals he covered the main points of the way he wanted a composition to be played. Then at the actual performance he expected his men to follow his beat, the sweeping gestures of his arms, the grimaces of his face, the swaying movement of his body and to learn from them the subtleties and details of interpretation he was seeking. Spontaneity, freshness, vitality, emotional intensity, power have been the hallmarks of Stokowski's greatness as a musical interpreter.

His greatest contribution has perhaps been in the area of modern music. It must be remembered that in 1912, and in the decade that followed, America heard very little new music. World premières were rare events. Program-making was in more or less of a rut, following familiar grooves. But from his very beginnings in Philadelphia, Stokowski made it his mission to bring twentieth-century music to a twentieth-century audience—over the violent protests of the orchestra's management; over the open opposition of the subscribers; over the hostility of local critics. In this battle—for this is actually what it turned out to be, year after year—Stokowski refused to yield his ground an inch. Each phase of contemporary musical thought was represented at his concerts, even works in the most radical, outlandish, and avant-garde idioms. The fact that today there is hardly a symphony orchestra anywhere in America that does not feature new music all the time—the fact that Leonard Bernstein can conduct in New York an entire series devoted to the most advanced tendencies in present-day music—all this is proof that in the end Stokowski proved victorious.

There is another proof of Stokowski's victory, and it lies permanently in the history book. The list of world or American premières which the Philadelphia Orchestra gave under Stokowski today reads like a Who's Who of twentieth-century music. There is hardly a front-ranking composer in our century who did not get a hearing in Philadelphia with Stokowski, and some of them were getting a hearing for the first time. There is hardly a major work in twentieth-century music which was not heard by Philadelphia audiences years ago. Here is just a sampling of the modern musical masterworks which Stokowski introduced to the United States: the last three symphonies of Sibelius; the third and fifth symphonies and *The Divine Poem* of Scriabin; Elgar's *Enigma Variations;* Rachmaninoff's Third Symphony and Fourth Piano Concerto; Manuel de Falla's *El Amor Brujo;* Stravinsky's *The Rite of Spring, Les Noces,* and *Oedipus Rex;* Shostakovich's First Symphony; Alban Berg's opera *Woz-*

zeck; Arnold Schoenberg's *Pierrot Lunaire* and *Kammersymphonie.*

So much for the Europeans. Stokowski was even more conscientious in promoting the interests of Americans. In his very first conducting post, in Cincinnati, he shocked his audience by offering an all-American program, something without precedent in the American symphony hall at that time. As the years passed, American works came thick and fast on his programs. Because of Stokowski, more than one present-day distinguished American composer was performed for the first time by a major symphony orchestra. Here are a few of the many prominent Americans who were performed by Stokowski when they were still comparatively obscure and neglected: Charles T. Griffes, John Alden Carpenter, Edgard Varèse, Aaron Copland, Wallingford Riegger, Henry F. Gilbert, Abram Chasins, Roy Harris, Harl McDonald.

Stokowski was born not in Poland, but in London, England; the year was 1882, *not* 1887 (as he long insisted), on April 18; he was baptized not Lionel Stokes but Leopold Bolesawowicz Stanislaw Anton Stokowski. His father was of Polish descent, and his mother was Irish; neither one was a musician.

Leopold Stokowski knew he would be a professional musician almost from the time he started studying the violin and piano in his fifth year. He first dreamed of becoming a conductor when he was seven. His initiation into the world of conducting came when he was only twelve—in a small opera house in a London slum where he was then working as rehearsal pianist and orchestral violinist. The opera house conductor had become ill, and nobody around seemed to know how to direct the performance. Little Leopold asked for the chance, got it, and apparently did well. In any event, once he had grasped baton in hand, and felt the exhilaration of drawing music from orchestra men and singers, he realized with finality that his future lay in conducting.

But before this happened he specialized on the organ, the only instrument to which he responded with anything like the excitement he later showed for the orchestra. His main music study took place at the Royal College of Music in London, under such renowned teachers as Sir Charles Stanford and Walford Davies; for a while, he also attended Queen's College at Oxford. His lifelong passion for the music of Johann Sebastian Bach was first aroused during these student days, and it became a fixation as he developed his organ virtuosity.

In 1900 he began his professional life in music through an appointment as organist of St. James's Church in the Piccadilly section of London. During this time he continued his music study with private teachers in Paris and Munich while on summer vacation. The rest of the year he learned by himself to play each instrument of the orchestra.

When he came to the United States in 1905 he assumed the posts of organist and choirmaster at St. Bartholomew's Church, Forty-fourth Street and Madison Avenue, in New York. He acquired a considerable following for his organ performance, and especially for his interpretations of Bach's music. But his success at the organ did not make him forget his ultimate goal. In 1908 he conducted several concerts with a minor London orchestra. This was all the experience he had had when in 1909 he received a call from Cincinnati to become principal conductor of its smphony orchestra.

That Cincinnati orchestra was being reorganized in 1909. Its directors, as impressed by Stokowski's dynamic personality as by his organ playing, suspected that here was a man able to breathe new life into a dying institution. Stokowski came to Cincinnati and forthwith left no doubt that his word would be the final law in all things pertaining to orchestral performances. The audience might prefer the familiar classics. Stokowski insisted upon playing new music and unfamiliar masterworks. His all-American program aroused a furor of protest from his audience as well as from the board of directors and the critics, and the auditorium for that concert was three-quarters empty. But this did not discourage Stokowski who flew into the eye of the hurricane by performing more and more American music as well as new European compositions. He also began taking his audiences severely to task for bad concert-hall manners. Disturbed one evening in 1911 by the continual rustling of programs while the music was being played, he stopped his orchestra, turned sharply around and shouted: "Please don't do *that!* We must have the proper atmosphere! We work hard all week to give you this music, but I cannot do my best, and our orchestra cannot do its best, without your help. I'll give you my best or I won't give you anything. It is for you to choose."

As the conductor grew increasingly uncompromising in his aim to give the best possible music in the best possible performances, the sparks of dissension began to fly. In two years, he had outgrown provincial Cincinnati, and he knew it. He needed a better orchestra, a more sophisticated audience and press, and greater freedom of activity if he was to carry out his mission and fulfil his ideals. When, therefore, he was offered the post of conductor of the Philadelphia Orchestra in 1912 he seized the opportunity. Despite the fact that the directors of the Cincinnati Symphony had fought him all the way in his innovations and revolutions, they now came to him pleading that he reconsider his decision, promising to comply with his every wish in the future. They could not conceive of any other conductor in Cincinnati but Stokowski. "Adjustments can always be made," the directors told him. Stokowski replied angrily: "Adjustments? What cannot be adjusted is the loss of my enthusiasm, which enthusiasm is absolutely necessary in the constructive work of building an orchestra!" At his final rehearsal in Cincinnati, a spokesman for the orchestra came forward with a promise that all musicians would henceforth cooperate fully with their conductor if Stokowski decided to stay on. Stokowski's only answer was: "Let's get on with our work today." Subscribers sent appealing letters to management and press. Stokowski ignored them. He had the Philadelphia Orchestra contract in his pocket. He was not only going eastward, but *also,* from the point of view of *his* career, upward.

The Philadelphia Orchestra was by no means a major symphonic organization in 1912, though it was superior to the one in Cincinnati. It was about ten years old when Stokowski arrived, and at that time it was generally regarded by its more distinguished competitors in New York and Boston as decidedly small-time. Philadelphia was also fully aware of the shortcomings of its concerts. That is why they lured Stokowski from Cincinnati. They had followed his activities in that city closely and had come to the realization that he was the kind of dynamic force able to vitalize and dramatize Philadelphia's musical life.

The Academy of Music was crowded to capacity when Leopold Stokowski gave his first concert in Philadelphia on October 11, 1912. Here is the way the critic of the *Public Ledger* described that debut: "Stokowski came forward with bowed head, evidently pondering the content of his musical message. Those who went forth to see a hirsute eccentricity

23

were disappointed. They beheld a surprisingly boyish and thoroughly businesslike figure who was sure of himself, yet free from conceit, who dispensed with the score by virtue of an infallible memory, and held his men and his audience from the first note to the last firmly in his grasp."

Stokowski's program comprised Beethoven's *Leonore Overture No. 3*, Brahms's First Symphony, Ippolitov-Ivanov's *Caucasian Sketches* (a "first" for Philadelphia) and Wagner's Overture to *Tannhäuser*. The critic for the *Public Ledger* described the performance as follows: "The new leader has been surprisingly successful in welding the several choirs into a single coherent entity. They played yesterday with a unity of purpose—particularly among the first violins—not usually attained until mid-winter. They brought out the full value of the lights and shadows. The climaxes were duly accentuated, the pianissimos with the utmost delicacy and refinement were contrasted with the full-throated polyphony . . . His gestures are graphic, the arcs and parabolas he describes tell of a kind of geometrical translation going on in his mind whereby he visualized the confluent rhythms in outward action . . . There is from the first to the last no langour or slackened moment; he directs with a fine vigor and intensity that mounts to ecstasy yet does not lose its balance or forget its sane and ordered method."

After the closing number, a floral wreath was carried to the conductor's dais. It was so huge that Stokowski was able to stand in it while responding to the tumultuous ovation the audience was giving him. This triumph was an omen of things to come at Philadelphia's Academy of Music. But not even the most rabid of Stokowski's admirers that day could have guessed the vistas of greatness this young, handsome, strong-willed, and electrifying conductor would open up for symphonic music in Philadelphia during the next quarter of a century.

The Stokowski years in Philadelpha were a shining epoch in American symphonic music, of a luster comparable to the Toscanini years in New York and the Koussevitzky years in Boston. The way in which Stokowski combined sensationalism with the soundest musical values helped to make symphonic music in Philadelphia an attraction that taxed the audience capacity at the Academy of Music concert after concert, year after year. And his adventurous program-making—at first without a parallel in the United States—built Philadelphia up into a major center of musical activity. Stokowski allowed nothing and no one to stand in the way of his progress as an artist and the progress of great music in his city. The cost of additional rehearsals, of paying top-flight artists to assume first-desk positions, of raising the pay of all the men in the orchestra so that they could devote their entire efforts to him—all this inspired a groan from the orchestra directors. But they paid the bills, however grudgingly, because there would have been no other way for them to keep their conductor.

In 1916, for example, Stokowski demanded and got an additional $14,000 to present a single composition—the American première of Gustav Mahler's monumental Eighth Symphony. This additional sum was needed because this work (dubbed "The Symphony of a Thousand Voices") required a greatly augmented orchestra, eight solo voices, a double chorus and a boys' choir. The director rebelled against spending so much money for the presentation of a work in which Philadelphia had no interest. But they surrendered in the end. Much to their surprise, this symphony proved so successful that Stokowski had to give nine performances in Philadelphia to meet the box-office demand; and he carried his huge army of singers and musicians to New York for a performance there. But beyond the fact that these concerts brought in a profit was the fact that they helped to focus the attention of the world on the Philadelphia Orchestra.

His demands on the men of the orchestra, the audience, and the orchestra managers grew increasingly severe. Just as he disregarded physical limitations when he rehearsed, just as he sidestepped the wishes of his audiences for the popular and the familiar, so he ignored budgets. Friction between himself and those with whom he worked was consequently unavoidable, and at times it reached the explosion stage. Such a point was reached in 1934 when Stokowski handed in his resignation. If it was calculated to establish once and for all who was the ultimate power in the Philadelphia Orchestra, this resignation succeeded completely. The directors were stunned by the prospect of losing Stokowski, who by now had become one of the greatest box-office attractions in American music. Where could they possibly find a replacement for Stokowski, and would his audience accept such a replacement? Rather than try to answer such vexing questions, the directors voted unanimously to confer on Stokowski the title of music director, which gave him full dictatorial powers.

Two years later Stokowski once again announced his resignation, to become effective in 1938. This time Stokowski meant it. He explained that he wanted more time for research, and he promised to return each year for a number of guest appearances.

The real reason why Stokowski decided to give up his post in Philadelphia was probably far different than the one he gave. It is possible that having soared as high as any conductor possibly could he was growing restless for new worlds to conquer. He was already looking longingly toward Hollywood where he hoped to bring great music to the screen. It is also possible that continual disagreements with the Philadelphia Orchestra management, particularly over the problem of all the new music he was continually performing, had exhausted his patience. Whatever the reason, he resigned his musical directorship in 1938. Until 1940 he continued to return to Philadelphia for guest appearances. Then after 1940 he was through with Philadelphia, at least for the next two decades. In February of 1960 he finally returned to the orchestra he had raised to such heights, and which had done him a similar service, for a number of concerts. This was an occasion to bring tears to the eyes of many, and to encourage shouts of welcome from all—as Stokowski walked briskly across the stage where more than twenty years earlier he had been the monarch of all he surveyed.

One of the reasons, Stokowski has always been addicted to food fads, physical exercises, and leading a carefully regulated daily life—and the reason why he always tried to strip five years off his age—has been his inordinate affection and admiration for youth. He wanted to keep young because he loved young people and understood them. And they understood him.

The youth concerts he had inaugurated in Philadelphia—one of America's first great orchestras to do so with its principal conductor—were extraordinarily successful because he knew how to communicate with young people, both in spoken words and in the music he played. Respecting the ability of young people to govern themselves, he enjoyed turning over to them the full administration of these youth concerts, having the youngsters plan the programs, write the program notes, handle the publicity, do the ushering, and staff the box office.

His interest in the young was one of the reasons why he always kept infusing new blood into the Philadelphia Orchestra. Some of those whom he hired were only in their late teens. When he detected conducting potential in one of these young musicians he did everything in his power to help him realize a career with the baton. Out of the ranks of the Philadelphia Orchestra have come a number of highly gifted conductors including Fabien Sevitzky, Saul Caston and Jacques Singer.

After leaving Philadelphia, Stokowski often appeared as guest conductor with leading orchestras all over the world. For a brief period in the middle 1940s he was the musical director of the Hollywood Bowl Concerts in Los Angeles, and in the middle 1950s he was the principal conductor of the Houston Symphony in Texas. But his major efforts as conductor were directed toward young people. He founded new orchestras where they could get experience. Working with young people provided him with a seemingly limitless source of joy and inspiration. It made him feel young, which was perhaps to be expected. What was less foreseeable was the way in which young people were energized by him. For time was unable to rob Stokowski of his extraordinary vitality, enthusiasms, capacity for hard and sustained work, and his ever inquisitive search for fresh and new paths in music.

Three times he assembled untrained and inexperienced young musicians into symphonic organizations which became under his skillful hands, and because of his magnetizing personality, music-making bodies commanding respect. The first time was in 1940 when he organized the All-American Youth Orchestra to provide young and unemployed musicians a chance to make music. Fifteen thousand young musicians came from every state for the auditions. This number was sifted down to about five hundred. Stokowski then traveled all over the country listening to each one and making his final choices. The average age of the musicians in the new orchestra was eighteen; two of the youngsters were only fourteen years old. After a number of preliminary concerts, Stokowski took his organization on a good-will tour of South America (with funds which came mainly from his own pocket). This journey was a triumph. Stokowski then brought his brood back to America for public concerts and recordings. In a short period of time, his orchestra had professional competence capable of presenting an exacting repertory. It bore the unmistakable Stokowski stamp, which meant that it was big-league.

Once again, in 1944, he founded an orchestra of comparatively inexperienced and non-professional material—the New York City Symphony. Young Leonard Bernstein, then still a musical neophyte, took over the musical direction of this organization in 1945, and kept it on a high standard until it passed out of existence in 1949 for lack of funds.

Eighty years old in 1962, Stokowski still had the will, vigor and idealism to build a new orchestra. This was the American Symphony, which gave its first concert in New York on October 15, 1962. It was formed, as Stokowski explained at the time, "to afford opportunity to highly gifted musicians regardless of age, sex, or color, and to offer concerts of great music within the means of everyone." After the first concert, a New York critic wrote rhapsodically: "Stokowski has done it again." Other critics called the performance a "phenomenon," described it as "full of imagination and genius" and commented that it "cast a spell." So successful did this new orchestra become that its second season was expanded from six to eight subscription concerts; the third season offered fourteen concerts; and the fourth season, twenty.

Once again youth was dominant in the Stokowski orchestra. About 70 percent of the personnel of the American Symphony was under thirty years of age. This factor, Emily Coleman explained in *The New York Times Magazine*, "contributes heavily to Stokowski's whole-hearted interest in the enterprise." Miss Coleman added: "After more than fifty years before the public, he has apparently found his own fountain of youth through the American Symphony Orchestra, an organization that has given him new listeners on whom to practise his legerdemain and a new outlet through which to spend the wealth of experience that has made a wiser, but not a sadder, man. People today are talking about Stokowski again, and nothing makes him happier."

EUGENE ORMANDY

[Born 1899]

WHEN LEOPOLD STOKOWSKI announced his resignation as musical director of the Philadelphia Orchestra in 1936, the question of succession became critical. For over two decades, Stokowski had been an idol in Philadelphia and New York. So completely, so inextricably had Stokowski identified himself with his orchestra that it was impossible to think of one without the other. The query was now frequently heard: Could the Philadelphia Orchestra survive without Stokowski?

Time and again great conductors have come and gone while the orchestras they left behind them survived and eventually continued to prosper. The consensus in Philadelphia and New York in 1936 was that there would always be a Philadelphia Orchestra, for Stokowski had built wisely and well. But it was obvious to one and all that the orchestra would survive and prosper only if another conductor could be found with some of Stokowski's musical endowments and personal appeal. He would have to be a conductor of world-fame—somebody, say, like Wilhelm Furtwaengler, Germany's great conductor, who (so rumor maintained) was ready and willing to take over the Philadelphia assignment.

When the announcement of Stokowski's successor was

finally made, it caused consternation to some, shock to many. For the man chosen to succeed Stokowski was not a world figure like Furtwaengler, but a comparatively young man with little conducting background. He was Eugene Ormandy, whose early experiences as conductor had taken place not in the opera house or symphony hall as was to be expected, but—of all places!—in a motion picture theater and over the radio. This was the first time that anybody had graduated from radio and movie house to become eventually conductor of one of the world's greatest orchestras.

The skeptics (and they were legion) prophesied that young Ormandy would hardly survive a single season; that the audience, so long educated to the highest standards, would stay away from Ormandy's concerts in droves.

But a strange thing happened. The audiences kept coming to Ormandy's performances that first season, and concert after concert the Academy of Music remained full. Ormandy's programs were consistently fresh and inviting; in fact they were more varied than Stokowski's had been, by placing particular emphasis on a well-rounded classical repertory. At the same time, modern music was not neglected. And whatever Ormandy played showed authority and imagination.

This was no carbon-copy Stokowski—though the temptation for Ormandy must at first have been great to try to emulate some of the more sensational methods and idiosyncrasies that had made Stokowski such a spectacular attraction. By temperament modest and retiring, Ormandy shunned sensationalism. He had to win his audiences in his own way— simply, unaffectedly, quietly.

At rehearsals, his men were brought face to face with a soft-spoken workman who operated methodically and efficiently without losing either temper or good manners. What impressed the musicians particularly was the sure way in which Ormandy set about to do his job. Experienced or not, this man obviously had the orchestral literature well in mind and hand, and at the same time he possessed the means with which to handle an orchestra expertly.

At concerts, audiences saw a somewhat reserved, unostentatious musician who concerned himself with, and dedicated himself solely to, the music. No speeches à la Stokowski! No stirring of a hornet's nest with the branch of some provocative opinion! No undue theatricalism in the interpretations! It was obvious from Ormandy's first concert in his new post that he had no intention of buying success with counterfeit coin.

Ormandy survived that first season, and the season after that. In fact he survived not only to become musical director of the orchestra in 1938 but also, in time, to celebrate the thirtieth anniversary of his affiliation with the Philadelphia Orchestra (one of the longest tenures of a conducting post in performing history). The orchestra under his hands became a different instrument. The sensual, orgiastic sounds that Stokowski so liked to draw from the men had been replaced by a more mellow sound, an Ormandy sound, emphasizing the violins, since the violin was Ormandy's instrument. But if its sound became different under Ormandy, the orchestra's extraordinary virtuosity had lost not an iota of its perfection and brilliance.

With Ormandy, and with Stokowski, the Philadelphia Orchestra remained a staunch champion of new music—from the romantic effusions of Rachmaninoff and Howard Hanson to the avant-garde writings of Roger Sessions and Lukas Foss. Ormandy's premières and commissions over three decades represent some of the finest fruits of musical creativity the world over: new works (works now accepted as basic to the orchestral repertory) by composers like Samuel Barber, Bartók, Britten, Kodály, Hindemith, Milhaud, Piston, Prokofiev, William Schuman, Shostakovich, Virgil Thomson, and Vaughan Williams.

Under Ormandy, the Philadelphia Orchestra not only made extensive transcontinental and regional tours in the United States; it also traveled to Australia in 1944, England in 1949, and all of Europe in 1955 and 1958; during the last of these trips abroad it made its first appearance in the Soviet Union and in countries behind the Iron Curtain.

In addition, the Philadelphia Orchestra under Ormandy has become one of the most active and successful broadcasting and recording organizations in the world. Since 1944 orchestra and conductor have released almost three hundred longplaying recordings for Columbia, three of these topping the million-dollar mark in sales, a feat unequaled by any other symphonic organization. The Philadelphia Orchestra was the first major symphonic body to appear over TV—on the CBS network on March 20, 1948: One of its most memorable and historic TV appearances took place on the day that President John F. Kennedy was assassinated, a coast-to-coast performance of Brahms's *Requiem*. In 1961–62, the Philadelphia Orchestra under Ormandy presented a TV series of music by American composers entitled *Sound of America*, following it a year later with the TV series, *Sound of Genius*, and two years later with *The Magic Melody*.

Thirty years after he first assumed the conductor's post in Philadelphia, Ormandy is even more energetic, more indefatigable, more the personification of perpetual motion than the had been in 1936. Take, for example, the season of 1963–

34

64, a period when the orchestra still functioned on a thirty-seven-week season. Ormandy conducted 106 of the 161 concerts given by the orchestra—a Herculean undertaking entailing not only the giving of concerts, but also rehearsals, recording sessions, travel, and various public appearances. The season over by the end of May, Ormandy then led summer concerts at the new Jersey Tercentary Festival of Music, and at the Berkshire Festival at Tanglewood. In August, Ormandy and his orchestra embarked on a six-week transcontinental tour, during which he performed twenty-eight concerts in cities from coast to coast.

This program of activity had to be increased and intensified in 1965–66 because the orchestra now extended its season to fifty-two weeks (forty-eight weeks of employment, and four weeks of vacation). With the regular season in Philadelphia ended, the orchestra embarked on a five-week tour of South America (its first there), after which it came to Saratoga Springs, New York, its new summer home, to inaugurate the Performing Arts Festival which from then on became an annual event.

In short, there has been no retreat during Ormandy's regime. On the contrary—there have been advances of all kinds. This is what Irving Kolodin had in mind when he wrote an appreciative piece on the Philadelphia Orchestra in 1963. He said in the *Saturday Review*: "The Philadelphia Orchestra hasn't opened a new hall this year (like the Philharmonic), it doesn't have a new conductor (like the Boston), nor has its leader been honored with a cover story on a national news magazine (like the Cleveland). All it has done this past winter is to give the most concerts ever in the history of its visits to New York . . . of which four, five or six were, without question, the four, five or six most beautiful examples of

35

orchestral artistry heard this season. All of this . . . could have been written twenty-five or thirty years ago when the conductor was Leopold Stokowski. The remarkable thing is that it can still be written a quarter of a century later though the conductor has long since been Eugene Ormandy and the personnel is so completely regenerated that the members engaged by Stokowski are no more than minimal." Then Mr. Kolodin concluded: "Unlike other orchestras which have had ups and downs, rises and declines, brilliant periods followed by reorganizations, the Philadelphia has been Philadelphia for all the years since Stokowski began his work in 1912."

Ormandy has gathered many an honor in the thirty or so years he has been associated with the Philadelphia Orchestra. He has been acclaimed in all the music centers of the world, having appeared as guest conductor with the foremost symphonic organizations everywhere and at some of Europe's leading festivals. He has received about a dozen honorary doctorates. In 1945 he was given the Order of Merit by the Dominican Republic; in 1958, he was promoted to Commander of the French Legion of Honor, of which he had been made Officer in 1952; in 1955 he became a Knight of the Order of the White Rose in Finland. However great these and similar honors and tributes have been, I think that Irving Kolodin's accolade is perhaps the highest. It points up the salient fact that though the Philadelphia Orchestra had been one of the greatest in the world when Ormandy inherited it from Stokowski, it has remained on those heights ever since. And a greater accomplishment than this for any conductor it is difficult to conceive.

Eugene Ormandy was born in Budapest, Hungary, on November 18, 1899. He was a child prodigy as violinist, encouraged by a doting father (a dentist, by profession) who is said to have taught the child rhythm in the crib. At the age of one and a half, Eugene could identify some fifty musical compositions after listening only to a few measures. A few years later he revealed he had been born with perfect pitch: Taken to a violin recital, he was so disconcerted by the wrong note played by the performer that he yelled from his seat: "F-sharp, not F natural!"

Violin study began when he was four, on an eighth-size instrument built especially for him. A year later he became the youngest student ever to enter the renowned Budapest Academy. There his teacher was Jenö Hubay, one of the leading violin teachers of his generation. Ormandy had been named after Hubay, Jenö, being the Hungarian equivalent of Eugene. "My lessons with Hubay filled my days with work and with dreams," Ormandy later recalled. "My fingers were numb from the exercises of Kreutzer and Cramer and later the showpieces of Vieuxtemps and Sarasate." He learned so quickly and so well that when he was seven he could make his concert debut. At fourteen he became the youngest student every to receive a Bachelor degree in music from the Academy. About two years after that he also got a special decree from the Ministry of Education to get him that diploma because of his youth.

In 1919 Ormandy was made head of the master class in violin at the Budapest State Conservatory. But the concert stage was still his prime interest. He made a number of tours of Central Europe which were praised so highly that they convinced him he was ready for a virtuoso career. At this crucial period in his life he met an impresario who offered to arrange an American tour. Giving up his teaching post, and selling all his belongings to pay for his fare to New York,

37

Ormandy set sail for the United States. He arrived in 1921, penniless, but with soaring hopes for the future.

Ormandy hardly had the time to unpack when he discovered to his horror that the impresario had exaggerated his managerial capacities. Not only was there no tour in the works, but the manager had failed to arrange a single concert. In fact, the manager had disappeared into thin air. Thus Ormandy found himself in a strange land without relatives, friends, or funds.

One day, he was standing on the corner of 50th Street and Broadway with only five cents in his pocket, and a stomach rumbling with hunger. He was debating whether to spend that last coin on some food or to use it for fare back to his room. Suddenly an acquaintance from Budapest crossed his path and recognized him. That man was Erno Rapee, the musical conductor of the Capitol Theatre, one of New York's leading movie palaces. The first thing Rapee did was to lend Ormandy some money. The second was to urge him to come to the theater and become a violinist in the Capitol Theatre orchestra.

Ormandy was only a week in that violin section when he was promoted to concertmaster. He also played violin solos on a weekly radio program originating from the Capitol Theatre. Then, one evening, the conductor of the Capitol Theatre orchestra became ill and was not able to conduct the performance, which consisted of a movement from Tchaikovsky's Fourth Symphony. Ormandy stepped from his concertmaster's seat and conducted without rehearsal. "I discovered a new instrument," Ormandy says of that experience, "richer and fuller than the violin—the orchestra." This impressive exhibition brought him a conducting job. For over seven years, Ormandy served as principal conductor of the Capitol

Theatre orchestra, directing an extensive repertory. "We played good music, movements from great symphonies, and even such modern classics as Richard Strauss's *Till Eulenspiegel*. And, mind you, since each week we performed every work about twenty times, we had an almost incomparable opportunity to learn the music with intensive minuteness. After all, a conductor of a symphony orchestra does not play, say, *Till Eulenspiegel* twenty times in as many years. And so, by conducting each masterpiece twenty times or so in succession over a period of several days—and doing this for years—I acquired a repertory, and acquired it by learning each note in the score by heart."

He now began acquiring a repertory in another way, too—by reading scores night after night the way some people read detective stories. From the beginning of his career as conductor, Ormandy possessed an extraordinary facility to read even the most complex orchestral music—to encompass the over-all design and proportions of a musical work without losing sight of details, and to comprehend almost by instinct the message of the composer. A fantastic memory also served him well. Once he read a score through he knew it by heart. And so, day after day, year after year, Ormandy created for himself a storehouse of musical masterpieces from which he could draw when the time came for him to become the conductor of a major symphony orchestra.

The work at the Capitol Theatre was arduous, seven days a week, with several performances a day. But Ormandy took his chores in stride not only because he loved conducting but also because he had the necessary physical stamina. Though a short man, standing only five feet four, he had a well-developed body with strong shoulders and chest and with the supple muscles of a trained athlete. This was the source of his

39

remarkable energy, both on and off the podium. Then, as later, he was a demon for hard work, and seemed indefatigable. Realizing that success as a conductor would depend almost as much on his physical as artistic resources, he had an athlete's respect for his body and refused to abuse it. He never touched tobacco nor drank intoxicating liquors: in fact he became intolerant of those who did. Attending a party, his indulgence would be a Hungarian raspberry syrup. He avoided rich foods, preferring a simple and nutritious diet to gourmet repasts. He kept regular hours at the modest apartment he maintained in New York with his wife, the former Steffy Goldner, a harpist in the New York Philharmonic Orchestra, whom he married on August 8, 1922.

A movie-house conductor does not command much respect among serious musicians. Nevertheless, Eugene Ormandy's performances at the Capitol Theatre began to attract attention. W. J. Henderson, distinguished music critic of the New York *Sun*, wrote an article praising not only the kind of music that could be heard at the Capitol Theatre but also the way it was played. This may have been the reason why, one day, Arthur Judson—the powerful concert manager—came to the theater to hear for himself. What he heard must surely have been impressive for then and there he signed Ormandy to a contract. Through Judson, Ormandy found opportunities to conduct outside the movie theater, first with a dance company, and then over the radio.

By 1929, Ormandy had become sufficiently convinced of his ability to make headway as a symphony conductor outside a motion-picture theater to give up his lucrative job at the Capitol Theatre for good. That summer he made a number of guest appearances at the Lewisohn Stadium in New York. During the summers of 1930 and 1931 he conducted at the

Robin Hood Dell in Philadelphia. He also conducted concerts regularly over the radio, through the facilities of the Columbia Broadcasting System.

What he now needed was that first big "break" to focus the limelight on him and convince the music world he was more than just a movie-house and radio conductor. That big "break" arrived in the fall of 1931 in Philadelphia. Toscanini had been contracted to direct several guest concerts with the Philadelphia Orchestra. A severe attack of neuritis compelled the Maestro to cancel his concert at the last moment. One after another conductors turned down an offer to appear as a Toscanini replacement, unwilling to invite unwelcome comparisons. Then, as Ormandy himself likes to tell the story, "someone called me on the telephone and said: 'Hello, is this Mr. Ormandy? This is Leopold Stokowski.' I thought it was my friend Alfred Wallenstein playing a joke, so I said: 'Ah, cut it out, Wally.' But the voice on the phone went on in a very dignified tone: 'Would you like to conduct the Philadelphia Orchestra in view of Mr. Toscanini's illness?' I couldn't believe it."

Ormandy's friends, even his manager, pleaded with him not to accept, convinced that at this sensitive juncture in Ormandy's career a fiasco in Philadelphia would have proved fatal. Philadelphia had grown up on the glamorous Stokowski. It was now expecting the legendary Toscanini. Their reactions to a Toscanini substitute who basically had had only radio and movie-house experiences would undoubtedly be one of disappointment if not outright antagonism. Ormandy thought the matter over carefully and came to the conclusion he could not avoid the challenge. If he *was* meant to be a symphony conductor this was as good a time as any to prove it, even with the odds against him. And so he called up Stokowski to accept the engagement.

His natural talent for conducting, his fine musicianship that avoided the obvious and the spectacular, his ability to project his personality, and the quiet dignity with which he presented the program all made a deep impression on the audience. It is possible that some had come into the auditorium to jeer; but at the end of the concert a good many rose to cheer.

On the strength of this splendid guest appearance Ormandy was appointed the following fall principal conductor of the Minneapolis Symphony. At that time the Minneapolis Orchestra had very little stature. Five years later, when Ormandy left Minneapolis to become first conductor of the Philadelphia Orchestra in succession to Stokowski, the orchestra in Minneapolis was one of America's twenty-five leading symphonic organization, good enough to make recordings for RCA Victor and to attract national interest.

Ormandy's work in Minneapolis also attracted national attention. He had proved that while his apprenticeship had taken place outside the concert hall, he was now a full-fledged symphony conductor. When, therefore, Stokowski decided to end his long and historic career at the head of the Philadelphia Orchestra, the directors (encouraged by Stokowski's enthusiasm) shrewdly decided to place the fate of their great ensemble in the young and energetic hands of a young conductor whose future promised so much. Ormandy's contract in Minneapolis still had a year to run, but the orchestra's directors generoulsy decided to release him.

In 1938, two years after he had become the principal conductor of the Philadelphia Orchestra, Ormandy's permanency was assured once and for all when he was given the Stokowski office of "music director." From then on, Ormandy's word in Philadelphia (like that of Stokowski before him) was law. His decisions, judgments, plans could no longer be vetoed.

In the thirty and more years Ormandy has been associated with the Philadelphia Orchestra he has not abused his high office. In Minneapolis he had often proved himself a tyrant (so much so that the musicians referred to him as "Little Caesar") In reshaping a fifth-rate orchestra into an important one, ruthless, dictatorial handling was in the cards without regard for personal feelings. But at Philadelphia, it was quite another story. Ormandy now had one of the greatest symphonic bodies in the world. Recognizing this fact, he was able to win his men over to him with geniality, tolerance, even familiarity. He has maintained such a relationship up to the present time. "I am one of you," he used to tell the musicians, and the musicians became convinced he meant it. "A conductor is only a musician," Ormandy now explains. "He is a father. The musicians tell me about their personal lives and problems and I help them. That's why they give everything."

Today, in the seventh decade of his life, he is as ambitious and as tireless as he was when he first assumed his office in Philadelphia. He still loves conducting, and does it even on holidays. His contract with the Philadelphia Orchestra does not permit him to make any guest appearances with other orchestras except when he is on his vacation. And so, Ormandy invariably uses vacation time to conduct great European orchestras and at leading European festivals. "I haven't rested in forty years," Ormandy recently told an interviewer. "I don't mind it. I love it! "

He has slowed down in several other ways, however. He used to have a passion for driving automobiles at breakneck speed. He no longer does so, especially after an automobile accident a few years ago had aggravated an old hip injury to give him a permanent, pronounced limp. He used to enjoy

Ping-pong which he played with almost professional speed and agility, but he has given up the game.

But the industry and passion and physical effort he expends on music-making remain undiminished. He still conducts with those broad sweeping gestures that make him seem on the podium so much taller than he really is. He is still indefatigable in the study of new scores, and still insists on committing to memory almost every piece of music he directs. Today, when he introduces a complex piece of new music he likes to have audiences sit in on the rehearsals. The result has exceeded Ormandy's expectation. He explains good-humoredly: "Before I used to get four hundred disagreeable letters after playing a difficult piece of new music. Now I get two hundred enthusiastic ones."

He is a grand seigneur, particularly when he receives visitors at his suite at the Bellevue-Stratford Hotel in Philadelphia which he has made his permanent home for the past decade and a half with his second wife, Greta. He likes to talk about himself, since he has never been guilty of false modesty. And since he enjoys to hear others talk about him, he thrives on flattery. But this same artist, with a healthy ego in his social life, can be almost self-effacing in his artistic calling. This happens whenever Ormandy plays a new work by a contemporary composer. He consults the composer on every detail of he score before he starts rehearsals, then invites the composer to come to rehearsal and make whatever suggestions are necessary, suggestions which Ormandy listens to patiently, ponders, and invariably accepts. Even after the composition has been played publicly, he consults the composer about any faults in the presentation that could be rectified in later performances. This humble approach to every new piece of music he conducts led the distinguished American composer,

Vincent Persichetti, to say: "It all contributes to giving the writer an inner satisfaction, a feeling that he not only has had his work played by the greatest orchestra of them all but he has found the best possible performance that the orchestra could have given it."

CHARLES MUNCH

[Born 1891]

O N APRIL 8, 1948, the directors and some of the leading patrons of the Boston Symphony Orchestra gathered for afternoon tea in the green room of the Boston Symphony on Huntington Avenue. Following tea, Serge Koussevitzky, the musical director of the orchestra, rose to make a brief announcement. He was retiring, and he had asked Charles Munch to take over the orchestra.

The announcement of Munch's appointment caused quite a stir in Boston's music circles—and with it a good deal of doubt and apprehension. For a number of years it had been a popular pastime in Boston to try guessing who would inherit Koussevitzky's baton. In all the choices for possible candidates, the name of Charles Munch rarely if ever appeared. For one thing, there were any number of conductors who were more popular and more appealing to Boston than Munch— this, in spite of the fact that between 1946 and 1948 Munch had made guest appearances in Boston and elsewhere that had inspired considerable praise. Nevertheless, conductors like Dimitri Mitropoulos, for example, or George Szell, or even Koussevitzky's pet protégé, Leonard Bernstein, seemed likelier candidates for the Boston post than Munch. In fact, Leonard

Bernstein had been a favorite in the betting, for by 1948 he had become one of the most highly publicized and adulated young conductors in America.

It is no secret that Munch's appointment caused deep concern in Boston. The musical cognoscenti raised the question whether a personality and an artistic temperament like those of Munch could possibly make any sort of a favorable impression in Boston after Koussevitzky. Munch was Koussevitzky's opposite in every conceivable way. Koussevitzky had been the autocrat given to violent tempers; the strong willed and opinionated dictator who brooked no opposition; the over-sensitized artist who was incapable of accepting unfavorable criticism gracefully. On the other hand, Munch was mild-mannered, affable, soft-spoken, a man who generated an air of friendliness and informality around him. Everybody who knew him called him "Charry" instead of Maestro or Dr. Munch, and it seemed perfectly natural to do so.

Munch's first rehearsal with the orchestra accentuated how far different he was from Koussevitzky. The men were sitting in their chairs rigid and tense as had been their custom at Koussevitzky's rehearsals, when Munch mounted his podium. Munch smiled gently. "Messieurs," he said softly, "relax!" He then made a little speech—in a broken English generously spiced with French words and phrases—in which he promised to do all he could to keep the great Boston Symphony on that high perch to which Koussevitzky had brought it. But, he added, he hoped that there would be "joy" as they worked together in making music. Before that first rehearsal ended, the musicians were completely won over to their new, kindly maestro. Not once had he raised his voice above a speaking volume. When he made corrections there was kindliness in his eyes and a soft smile played on the corners of his lips. A warm bond of respect, admiration, even affection began to develop between orchestra and conductor. With Koussevitzky there had usually existed admiration and respect rather than affection.

Munch's rehearsing methods also provided a marked contrast to those of Koussevitzky. The latter had worked the men ruthlessly, laboring over phrase after phrase for several hours until every element of the composition had been scrutinized, studied, practiced, mastered, and perfected. Munch, however, operated in an almost casual way. He skipped nimbly from one part of of the score to another, just touching upon random pages or passages that needed special attention. He suggested, he urged, he pleaded, he explained—but he never drove. He used poetical images and picturesque descriptive phrases to explain what he wanted. He told his men that one passage should "glide like a snake" while another should "float like smoke." To interpret a nocturnal episode he said that the music was "like the night . . . You are asleep . . . A tiny bit of sunshine comes through." His men soon came to see that he was just about the "most economical rehearser" they had ever experienced. When he was satisfied, he dismissed the orchestra, even long before the actual scheduled rehearsal period had ended. Munch was convinced that too much rehearsing robbed a performance of freshness and spontaneity, two virtues he regarded more highly than perfection of execution. In fact, some of his work as interpreter was done at the concert itself, his gestures shaping and carving the music as if it were a piece of clay in the hands of a sculptor. As Hope Stoddard wrote: "His gestures are amazingly articulate: his crouching back and drawing the men towards himself as if on reins of persuasion; a sudden plummeting of the hands for silence; a solicitous pointing; an urging sweep. Everything is of an appealing rather than a dictatory nature." Time and again he would emphasize that "music must breathe," that it was a "living thing." To work it over note by note, he maintained, was to "torture it to death." Overworking an orchestra, he insisted, only invited weariness and often led to stilted, lackluster performances. "The orchestra," he once said, "is not a docile or mechanical instrument. It is a social body, a collection of human beings. It has a psychology and reflexes. It can be guided, but it must not be offended."

Thus he radically changed the relationship between conductor and orchestra that had previously existed in Boston. He introduced a new kind of performance spontaneity, a new quality of orchestral sound. With Koussevitzky, performances had been passionate, intense, luscious. With Munch they became subdued, with the kind of dry tone European orchestras favored. Relaxation and calm had displaced nervousness and excitement. "No longer do the strings melt with Koussevitzkian emotion," said Harold Rogers in *The New York Times*. "No longer did the choirs blend and swell to rotund radiance. . . . The strings were drier, brighter. Each choir spoke in its characteristic way, coexisting but not fraternizing with the orchestra. Details stood out in crystalline focus."

During Munch's first season there were a few in the audience who were displeased with what they heard, preferring Koussevitzky's febrile kind of performances to Munch's sober ones. In fact there were many in Boston who felt that the entire music season had grown bland. With his inflammable, provocative ways, Koussevitzky had helped to keep the musical atmosphere in Boston continually electric. Munch, however, was too withdrawn, retiring, diplomatic, and unargumentative to arouse controversy or attract publicity.

But the consistently high standards of Munch's concerts won out over extraneous and meretricious considerations—and won out so completely and decisively that Munch was kept in Boston for thirteen seasons, the longest period any conductor had held the job there with the exception of Koussevitzky himself.

Munch conducted his first orchestral concert comparatively late in his life. He was past forty at the time. Up to his fortieth year he had made his living as a violinist.

He was born on September 26, 1891, in the Alsatian city of Strasbourg, which at that time was under German rule. He was the fifth of six children, an austere Protestant household whose head was the founder of the St. Guillaume Choir and professor of organ at the Strasbourg Conservatory. Dr. Albert Schweitzer—the world-famous humanitarian and Bach specialist—was a distant relative of the family.

Religion and church was one of the cornerstones of the Munch family. Music was another. Since both parents were highly musical, all children received formal instruction early. The making of music—like the worship of God—was basic to family routine. In the winters, the family gave performances of Bach cantatas in the living room. In the summers—spent at a country place in the Vosges—the family played chamber music. The sound of music echoed so frequently in the Munch home that the place was dubbed by the neighbors "the music box."

Charles' first ambition lay not in music but in locomotives. When he was six he knew the exact time every express train roared into the Strasbourg station. His greatest pleasure came from watching the international trains pour into the station. But while dreaming about locomotives, he studied music formally and intensively. In early boyhood he attended the Strasbourg Conservatory where one of his teachers was Hans Pfitzner, the distinguished German composer. The boy Munch played the violin in an orchestra conducted by his father, and at times he played the organ in church. The organ was his particular favorite. "Before those keyboards," Munch later recalled, "I felt almost like a demigod, holding in my hands the reins that controlled the musical universe."

Despite his partiality for the organ, Munch specialized in the violin. After receiving his Conservatory diploma in that department, Munch came to Paris in 1912, and found a small flat on the Île de la Cité near Notre Dame Cathedral. He now took violin lessons from one of France's most distinguished teachers, Lucien Capet. Munch was making excellent headway, and beginning to contemplate a virtuoso career, when World War I exploded over Europe. On the eventful 1914 day that war came, Munch was visiting his family in Strasbourg. The frontiers of Alsace and France were closed down permanently. As a native of Strasbourg, Munch was mustered into the German Army, where he served as sergeant gunner. He was gassed in Peronne, wounded at Verdun, and finally demobilized in Cologne.

The war over, Munch returned to his native city. By temperament, nature, outlook, personal philosophy, and patterns of behavior Munch had always been more French than German. This fact was strengthened during his two-year residence in Paris. With Strasbourg French territory after World War I, Munch could now become a French citizen. He was never again to consider himself anything but a Frenchman.

He earned his living playing violin in, then serving as concertmaster of, the Strasbourg Orchestra, and by serving as professor of the violin at the Conservatory. But he was already beginning to dream of becoming a conductor, and he did whatever he could to prepare himself for the time when such a dream could be translated into reality. He studied the techniques, methods, and interpretations of the two conductors most active in Strasbourg: Guy Ropartz of the Strasbourg Orchestra and Paul Bastide of the Strasbourg Opera. He was always head deep in orchestral scores.

It was some time, however, before he got his first chance to hold baton in hand. This happened in Leipzig, the German city to which Munch had come in 1926 to fill the concertmaster's chair with the historic Gewandhaus Orchestra, then led by Wilhelm Furtwaengler. Munch's activities in Leipzig included playing the violin in a small ensemble that accompanied performances of Bach's choral works at St. Thomas's Church—the very church where the great Johann Sebastian had once been employed as cantor. A day before one of these choral performances, the regular conductor became ill. Munch was recruited as a substitute. He memorized the music during the night and the next day gave a creditable account of himself in his conducting debut. Soon after that he found a second chance to conduct. The Leipzig Gewandhaus Orchestra was offering a historical series. One of these concerts represented the eighteenth century and required the concertmaster to direct the orchestra from his place at the first desk, with movements of head and shoulders, or with violin and bow when he was not playing the violin, as was habitual in bygone years.

In spite of these apprentice adventures, conducting for Munch lay very much in the future. "I was lazy," was the way Munch liked to explain the years it took him to change from violin to baton, but in saying this he was merely facetious. The truth was he had a living to make, and playing the violin was the only way he could support himself. Another truth was that it required large funds to pave the way for a conducting career in Europe through the hiring of some major orchestra or through the founding of a new symphonic organization.

Munch acquired such financial resources after marrying Genevieve Aubry, granddaughter of one of the founders of Nestlé, the famous Swiss manufacturer of chocolate. Munch had first met her when he lived in Paris between 1912 and 1914. Young, handsome, cultured, debonair, he had little difficulty in stirring her interest. During World War I they maintained contact through correspondence, with the help of the International Red Cross. After the war they were able to meet again, when their friendship blossomed into love.

In 1929, the musical authorities in Leipzig informed Munch he would not be permitted to retain his post of concertmaster with the Gewandhaus Orchestra unless he renounced his French citizenship and became a German again. This Munch refused to do. He left his job and came to Paris. At this crossroads in his career, Genevieve Aubry provided the funds with which to hire the Paris Symphony Orchestra for Munch's conducting debut in France. That concert took place on November 1, 1932, and was successful. Munch conducted several other orchestral concerts in France (all paid for by Genevieve) including such distinguished orchestras as the Lamoureux and the Straram. During the same period—in 1933—he and Genevieve were married.

In 1935, Munch founded his own symphony orchestra, calling it the Paris Philharmonic. He led it for three seasons in distinguished concerts, mainly of contemporary music. This was the period when he first emerged as an eminent interpreter of the French music of the past, particularly the music of Hector

Berlioz of which he became an interpreter second to none. Consequently, when one of the most important conductorial posts in Paris was left open, that of the Paris Conservatory Orchestra, Munch was chosen to fill the job. He conducted the orchestra for the next eight years with such distinction that he was invited all over Europe to appear in guest concerts.

His working habits, crystallized during those eight years and rigidly adhered to from then on, were described by him in the following way: "In the morning my mind is still fresh and everything seems to come easily and quickly. This is the best time to rehearse. Afternoons must be kept free. This is the time for receiving young composers looking for sponsors, soloists come for advice and the time for reading new scores and making programs. For careful study of scores I am performing I prefer the silence of the night when I get my second wind and the music engraves itself more quickly on my memory. The senses are sharpened by the day's excitement, and, most important, I know that nothing will disturb the solitude, peace, and silence, which are so rare and precious."

He stayed on in his job as conductor of the Paris Conservatory Orchestra during World War II, even after the Nazis marched into Paris. He felt that his countrymen now needed the solace and inspiration of great music more than ever; that through the presentation of French music, something of the soul and spirit of his country could be kept alive even while enemy flags were flying in Paris. However, he stubbornly refused to accept any assignment the Nazis offered him to conduct for the Germans, nor would he work with avowed collaborationists; the latter was the reason why he turned down the post of principal conductor at the Paris Opéra. He also defied Gestapo orders to purge his orchestra of those who, in Nazi estimation, were politically suspect. In addition to all this, he turned over his entire salary to the Resistance movement. He even allowed his house to become a station in the "underground railway" devised by the Resistance to help Frenchmen, in danger of Gestapo arrest, to escape from Paris.

The war ended, Munch assumed a place of first importance among Europe's conductors. He became the first Frenchman since the war to lead concerts in England. Then he toured the rest of Europe, the Near East, and South America. And finally he came for the first time to the United States. This happened in 1946 when he was invited to be a guest conductor of the Boston Symphony. He made his American debut in Boston on December 27, 1946, in an all French program that included two works new to the United States, one of these being Arthur Honegger's *Symphony for Strings*. Less than a month later he was heard in New York for the first time, directing the New York Philharmonic in a program predominantly French, featuring the American première of Honegger's Third Symphony. "It was evident," wrote Olin Downes in *The New York Times*, "that we had with us a superb musician. . . . Back of his qualities as a conductor—his masterly treatment of phrase, his exceptional range of sonorities, from the nearly inaudible pianissimo to the fortissimo that is so brilliant yet not too hard, the complete flexibility of beat and capacity, when that is desirable, for romantic rhetoric—are Mr. Munch's temperament and imagination."

Munch returned to the United States in 1948, this time bringing with him the National Radio Orchestra of France for its first tour of America. The superior qualities of his workmanship and style, and the finely chiseled contours of his over-all projection, became even more strikingly evident now that Munch was directing a French orchestra. It was probably on the strength of his personal successes on this coast-to-coast tour, and the appeal his kind of playing had for Americans everywhere, that led to his appointment that same year as the new musical director of the Boston Symphony.

After his first two seasons in Boston, Munch won his audiences so completely that it became obvious he could keep his job as long as he wished. Naturally, not only the sound of the orchestra changed with Munch and the personality of the symphonic interpretations. The programs also were different, since Koussevitzky's interest in Russian music was superseded by Munch's preference for French composers. But Munch, like Koussevitzky, was an advocate of new music, and under Munch the Boston Symphony remained a faithful barometer of what modern music was achieving. During his regime, Munch played 168 modern works, thirty-six by Americans; there were thirty-nine world premières, seventeen American premières, and thirteen Boston premières.

One of Munch's innovations was to intitiate open rehearsals to provide audiences with the opportunity to see how a piece of music was prepared. At first there were only five such events, but they grew so popular that in time this number was doubled. Today open rehearsals is something of a Boston institution.

Something else Munch was able to realize, something for which Koussevitzky had hoped yearningly for many a year without being able to realize it: bringing the wonderful Boston Symphony to Europe. This goal was finally realized in 1952 when the Boston Symphony under Munch made its first foreign invasion by performing in England, France, Holland, Belgium, and Germany. It was a journey paved with triumph from first to last, attended by heads of State, political dignataries, cultural leaders. Public ovations vied in intensity with

critical accolades in acclaiming the orchestra and its conductor. For Munch himself the high point of this tour was his return to his native city of Strasbourg where he could now
reveal himself at the height of his musical powers, and at the
head of one of the world's noblest symphonic institutions.
As Cyrus Durgin reported back to Boston: "When the capacity audience in Strasbourg's Salle de Palais des Fêtes let loose
with a storm of applause, that moment was perhaps the cul-
mination of a lifetime of music-making for Charles Munch. I
was able to see him, from a vantage point backstage, as he conducted the final number, Brahms's great and noble Fourth
Symphony. There was something almost transfigured in the expression on his face." A critic for *Les Dernieres Nouvelles
d'Alsace* wrote: "After the concert it looked as though the
whole audience, trembling with joy after what they had
heard, would strew his path homeward with roses."

After that, Munch brought the Boston Symphony on two
more foreign tours. In 1956 the organization was one of the
principal attractions at the world-famous Edinburgh Festival
in Scotland. This was also the tour in which musical history
was made, when the Boston became the first American orchestra to play in the Soviet Union. This Soviet debut took
place in Leningrad on September 6, 1956, in a program that
included Beethoven's *Eroica Symphony*, Walter Piston's
Sixth Symphony and Ravel's *Daphnis and Chloe*, Suite No. 2.
In a cable to *The New York Times*, William J. Jorden described this special event as follows: "A capacity audience of
about two thousand crowded into the concert hall of the Leningrad Conservatory to hear the Americans perform. The re-
ception given by Leningrad officialdom and music lovers
was warm and enthusiastic. Soviet and United States flags
grouped together above the orchestra, and this unaccustomed

sight seemed to symbolize the power of great music to bring peoples together whatever their other differences. . . . The all-white concert hall, with massive colonnades, red velvet portieres and gold and crystal chandeliers provided an impressive setting for this first performance by a Western symphony within the borders of the Soviet Union. . . . The 105-member orchestra surprised its audience by opening the program with the Soviet national anthem. There was a murmur, part amazement, part pleasure, as the audience rose to its feet. It remained standing for the American anthem. . . . Prolonged applause and cheers led Mr. Munch to play an encore, unusual for the Boston Orchestra. It was *The Sorcerer Apprentice* by Dukas. . . . The enthralled crowd stood and applauded wildly. . . . Even after the orchestra had left the stage, rhythmic clapping continued. . . . Grigoriev Rabinovich, conductor of the Kirov Opera Company, called the performance 'tremendous.' "

The Boston made one more triumphant foreign tour under Munch. In 1960 it visited the Far East, Australia, and New Zealand. After that Munch remained the orchestra's musical director up through the 1962 Berkshire Music Festival. The demands made by the Boston Symphony on a musical director, Munch felt strongly, were too exacting and too strenuous to be borne by a man past his seventieth birthday. The time had come for a younger musician to take over.

Charles Munch kept himself even more aloof from Boston society than his distinguished predecessor, Serge Koussevitzky, had done. Six foot tall, handsome, and the last word in courtly manners, Munch might easily have become something of a matinee idol in Boston but for the fact that he was reserved and shy. As *Time* once explained: "Like many another native of Alsace, Charles Munch is a composite of the characteristics of both France and Germany. In him the French bon vivant shines only dimly through a fog of German *Weltschmerz;* he enjoys life but seldom seems basically happy."

He occupied a large house on Brush Hill in Milton, eight miles from Boston. It was his haven of seclusion, a place in which to rest and work rather than a setting in which to entertain guests at cocktail parties and dinners. Each morning after breakfast he could be found taking a stroll through the neighborhood with his Welsh terrier, Pompey. This, and an occasional indulgence in golf, were just about his only forms of physical exercise. Later on in the morning he would be occupied with rehearsal in Boston. Afternoons he rushed back to Brush Hill Road. "Only when he reaches the sanctuary of his second-story study," *Time* has explained, "with Roger, his chauffeur-valet of twenty years' service, hovering around him does he seem to draw a relaxed breath." Much of the afternoon was devoted to studying scores. Evenings were spent quietly, most often only with his wife, but at times with one or two close friends; Munch disliked going to parties as much as he disliked giving them. At dinner, the cuisine was, to be sure, French; his favorite dishes were pot au feu or kidneys cooked with Chablis, supplemented of course, by the proper wines. Vacation time was spent in Paris where the Munches maintain a fourteen-room apartment near the Bois de Boulogne. That Paris apartment, now that Munch has left Boston —and now that his conducting chores are confined exclusively to guest appearances around the world—is his main retreat. Here he finds the time to pursue more actively such favored extra-musical interests as reading books on philosophy and classical literature, the study of Egyptology, and the collection of *objets d'art.*

ERICH LEINSDORF

[Born 1912]

ONE DAY IN 1961 Erich Leinsdorf was invited to have
lunch with Henry Cabot, president of the board of trustees of
the Boston Symphony. Leinsdorf came expecting nothing
more than a pleasant noonday exchange of ideas and opinions
on matters musical, and possibly a discussion about the activities and achievements of the Boston Symphony. But the lunch
had not progressed half an hour when Cabot informed Leinsdorf he wanted him to become a new musical director of the
Boston Symphony, in succession to Charles Munch. Being
offered on a platter what so many musicians would regard as
possibly the most desirable symphonic post in the world was
so unexpected, so beyond Leinsdorf's wildest hopes and ex-
pectations, that only after he had come home from lunch did
he realize he had forgotten to accept! He sat down and
despatched a brief note to Cabot reading: *"In general, when
one is invited, one should reply. Since you invited me, I just
want to tell you, 'Thank you, I accept.'"*

For the audiences of the Boston Symphony the presence of
Erich Leinsdorf on the conductor's platform represented a
new musical experience. For a quarter of a century the concerts had reflected the mercurial Russian personality of Serge

60

Koussevitzky; naturally, the Russian impress on Koussevitzky's performances and programs was strong and inescapable. Then came Charles Munch, whose decade or so of orchestral music in Boston helped to endow orchestra, programs, and performances with an equally unmistakable French identity.

With Leinsdorf, a different kind of musical personality was in evidence, a strongly Germanic personality. What we mean by this is not merely an emphasis on Austrian and German symphonic literature in the same way that Koussevitzky had been partial to Russian music and Munch to French. We mean much more than this. We mean the application of an over-all Germanic approach to music and music-making, radically different from the emotional, nervous ways of a Koussevitzky or the genial, gracious, well-assured methods of a Munch.

For though he is Austrian by birth, Leinsdorf is thoroughly German in musical and intellectual processes. He has the Germanic love for thoroughness, precision, and military discipline. He has the German fetish for organization and punctuality. They say of Leinsdorf that he always knows what he is doing or where he is going, and how long he will take to get there, down to the split second. If his car is expected at eight in the evening, say, he will be sure to put one foot out of his door at 7:59. "He's tremendously organized, a sort of musical computer," is the way Milton Esterow has described him. "There is this tremendous self-discipline."

Leinsdorf also has the Germanic respect for the intellect. His ideas about any piece of music are all meticulously analyzed and catalogued long before he comes to rehearsal. This is the reason why he conducts from memory, and why he so often even dispenses with the score in complex modern musical compositions. Every "i" in the music is forcefully dotted in his mind, and every "t" crossed. "I never expected to find a conductor who knows my own score better than I do," said the distinguished American composer Walter Piston after Leinsdorf had rehearsed and conducted his Seventh Symphony from memory. Leinsdorf leaves nothing either to chance or spontaneity. It is characteristic of his way of doing things that immediately after he had accepted the Boston Symphony post, he worked out in the most minute detail every practical aspect of his entire first season, including each of the programs.

Few conductors go through Leinsdorf's kind of exhaustive preparation for every concert, a preparation that has to work out in essentials the logical reason for each and everything he does. John M. Conly wrote in *High Fidelity* magazine: "The whole essence and governance of the man is a driving, highly sensitized, integrated and clear-focused intellectuality, whose chief working abstracts are relationships, proportion and harmony . . . A consummate musician like Leinsdorf must almost of necessity be philosophically holistic. This is a term coined by biologists and it denotes simply the viewing of an organism or a process as a whole, as the continuing sum of *all* its active parts. For organism or process, read historical event, man, orchestra, oneself—but centrally, here, music."

Fastidious, thorough, all-embracing preparation is probably the keyword to Leinsdorf's artistic personality. Characteristic of the lengths to which he goes in preparing his concerts is the way he rehearsed a group of empty chairs when he was working on the American première of Benjamin Britten's monumental *War Requiem*. The reason why Leinsdorf did this was because certain portions of the work called for a different seating arrangement in the orchestra than usual and Leinsdorf wanted to make sure he was as completely familiar with this new placement as he was with the music. There is always a sound explanation, carefully thought-out beforehand, for everything Leinsdorf does—and he expects the same response from the first-desk men when they wish to adopt a viewpoint of their own. When their point of view makes sense, he yields; otherwise he demands obedience.

Thoroughness is another keyword in Leinsdorf's character. It has been this way with him from the dawn of his career. As an apprentice he used to memorize all of Beethoven's string quartets because he felt they might provide a key to the better understanding of the symphonies and *Fidelio*. At nineteen he studied and mastered the Italian language because he wanted all the better to comprehend Italian operas, realizing that translation was a poor substitute for the original. When, as a young man in Salzburg, he was called upon to help rehearse Wagner's music drama *The Mastersingers* for Toscanini, he made his own piano arrangement of the huge score, memorized it, and thus was able to coach his singers without consulting the printed page. As a conductor at the Metropolitan Opera he would, in numerous private sessions, always try to get a picture of the *total* personality of each singer in the cast explaining that "one cannot cast only by voice; I view opera as a totality." In fact, he views all of music as a totality, and if he can be made to understand a score better by reading up on metaphysics, philosophy, religion, history, and so forth, he does not hesitate to do so.

Leinsdorf seeks technical perfection, of course. He is too much a stickler for musical accuracy to allow any sloppiness. "I like to have the right note played in the right place," he has explained. Nevertheless, once the right note is where it belongs, Leinsdorf's work first begins, whereas with a good many conductors it ends there. Accuracy can never be an end itself for him. Once accuracy has been achieved, Leinsdorf must try to comprehend and bring to life the dreams and visions of the composer. Leinsdorf, who always admired Bruno Walter greatly and learned much from that distinguished conductor, believes as Bruno Walter did when he said: "To know Beethoven, you must know *Hamlet* and Goethe."

"Leinsdorf's high humanism," says John M. Conly, "shows in endless cordial patience with his musicians' problems . . . but probably even better in his playing of the music he loves best, the tall and radiant classical symphonies. One need only cite, or urge hearing, the poignant glory of the *Eroica* funeral march, or the coruscant, swelling surge of Schubert's cosmic paean, the C major Symphony, as they awake at his hands. Call it dramatic; whatever it is, it is power. His Mozart is like living grass."

Though he works the orchestra men long and hard, and with dictatorial severity, he commands respect, even affection. An orchestra bitterly resents being driven only when it feels the conductor does not know in his own mind what he wants. But when a conductor has a definite and clear technical and interpretative goal in mind—a goal he has clarified for himself long before rehearsal time—and knows the best and shortest way to reach that goal, musicians can be tolerant not only of long hours but also of bitter harangues. Especially if the men know that their conductor respects them as musicians! In an article in the *Atlantic Monthly*, Erich Leinsdorf wrote: "In music, the leader—and that is precisely what the conductor is—finds himself in control of very highly skilled people whose excellence in their special fields must always be respected. Yet rehearsals involve so much criticizing and suggesting, prodding and coaxing by the conductor that they can easily become wrangles. It is here that sensitivity, tact, and au-

LEOPOLD STOKOWSKI

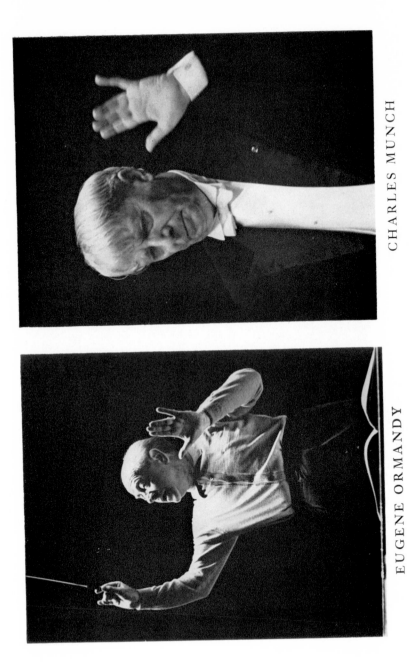

CHARLES MUNCH

EUGENE ORMANDY

ERICH LEINSDORF

OTTO KLEMPERER

GEORGE SZELL

New York Philharmonic

LEONARD BERNSTEIN

WILLIAM STEINBERG

JOSEF KRIPS

HERBERT VON KARAJAN

ZUBIN MEHTA

LORIN MAAZEL

thority come into play." From his very first day with the Boston Symphony, Leinsdorf brought with him sensitivity, tact, and authority. No matter how hard he pressed his men, they were on his side. In preparing an article on Leinsdorf for *High Fidelity* magazine, John M. Conly interviewed some of the members of the Boston Symphony to get their reactions to their new conductor. "They all told the same story. This was: they now had a leader, a surely great man, of extraordinary strength, skill and understanding, whom they liked (almost fiercely) and who (very touchingly) they were sure liked them. They seemed amazed at Leinsdorf, as if he were too good to be true. Two of them used the word 'Olympian,' which I am sure is not much bandied about in Boston."

When a great orchestra like the Boston Symphony, and a great conductor like Erich Leinsdorf are so attuned to each other, the inevitable result is musical performances of the highest order. The Boston Symphony is on the threshhold of still another great epoch in its already rich history.

Erich Leinsdorf was born in Vienna on February 4, 1912. His father, an amateur pianist, died when Erich was only three. The mother not only took over the responsibilities of supporting her family but also the duty of directing Erich to music, for which he had shown remarkable aptitude from earliest childhood. He was five when his mother began giving him piano lessons. These were continued with Hedwig Kanner-Rosenthal (wife of the world-famous piano virtuoso Moriz Rosenthal), one of Vienna's most distinguished piano teachers. When he was thirteen, Erich added the study of cello, theory, and composition to that of the piano.

Though he was making remarkable progress in music he had no idea at first of becoming a professional musician. As he told an interviewer: "Up to my fifteenth year I was in doubt that I was going to be. I was interested in soccer. I played left fullback, and when I was tired of running I was the goalee. I had a very good kick with my left foot." By the time he was eighteen he had decided to become a musical performer, though he was not yet sure whether he would be a pianist or conductor. Not having reached this decision, he took courses at the University of Vienna in 1930 and completed his music study at the Vienna State Academy of Music in 1933.

Once out of school he found few openings awaiting him either as pianist or conductor. Austria was in the depths of a depression; anti-Semitism was poisoning the atmosphere. A young Jewish-born musician, however brilliant, found doors closed to him. About the only job Leinsdorf could get was to serve as an assistant conductor to a workers' chorus.

Refusing to accept total defeat, Leinsdorf walked 155 miles from Vienna to Salzburg, during the summer of 1933, to try attracting the interest and support of the great Bruno Walter, one of Europe's giant conductors. Dusty and tired though he was upon arriving at Salzburg, he walked straight into the festival theater where Walter was then in the process of rehearsing Beethoven's *Fidelio* for a festival performance. At one point in the rehearsal, Walter was busily engaged in consultations with one of the singers. Leinsdorf chose that moment to seat himself at the piano on the stage when he played the Beethoven score from memory at the very point at which the rehearsal had been interrupted. This demonstration made a deep impression on Walter who hired young Leinsdorf as his assistant.

That same winter, Toscanini came to Vienna as guest conductor of several symphony concerts. Leinsdorf sat in on one of the rehearsals where he overheard the manager complaining that a pianist could not be found for Kodály's *Psalmus Hungaricus* which Toscanini was featuring. Leinsdorf offered his services, maintaining he knew this music well. When he played for Toscanini, the Maestro smiled broadly and remarked: "Very good, indeed." Not only did Toscanini engage Leinsdorf to play the piano part at the concert but he also invited him to return to the Salzburg Festival the following summer to help him prepare their opera productions.

To assist Toscanini and Bruno Walter in rehearsing operas at Salzburg was a prodigious task which young Leinsdorf took in his stride. He had to be in three or four different places at the same time in a single afternoon—practicing with the orchestra in one place; directing a chorus in another; coaching singers in a third; consulting the stage director in the fourth. He was able to juggle the schedule so that he could attend to all these duties, and to several others in the bargain. People in Salzburg used to say of Leinsdorf that he had the talent to be everywhere at the same time, always in full command of the job that had to be accomplished. He traveled from one place to the next sometimes by bicycle, sometimes by foot, and would hardly have the time to catch his breath when he threw himself into his work with the enthusiasm and freshness of one who was just beginning his day. Toscanini told some of his friends that summer that Leinsdorf's preparations had been so careful, studied, and exhaustive that when he himself was ready to take over all he had to do was "just make music."

Leinsdorf's goal was the Vienna State Opera. Toscanini and Bruno Walter both recommended him highly for a conducting post there, but the violent anti-Semitic feeling then prevailing in Vienna, and particularly at the Opera, made him unacceptable. But Leinsdorf did find opportunities to conduct outside Vienna. During the next two summers he assisted at the Salzburg Festivals besides helping out at the May Music Festival in Florence in May 1935. In the fall and winter of 1936 he led concerts in Bologna, Trieste, and San Remo. When I visited Italy at that time, one Italian musician told me: "Remember Leinsdorf. He reminds us all here of Toscanini when Toscanini started out as a conductor in Italy."

Lotte Lehmann, one of the word's greatest singers and a star of the Salzburg Festival, spoke about Leinsdorf to Artur Bodanzky, then the main conductor of German operas at the Metropolitan Opera in New York. Bodanzky, in turn, put in a good word for Leinsdorf with the Met's general manager, Edward Johnson. The result was a conducting contract for the Metropolitan Opera, Leinsdorf's first important permanent conducting assignment. He had trouble getting into the United States because of passport and visa difficulties, but the help of a young Congressman was enlisted to make the necessary arrangements. The Congressman's name was Lyndon B. Johnson.

Leinsdorf made his American debut on January 21, 1938, in Wagner's *The Valkyries*. Not yet twenty-six, Leinsdorf seemed that evening more like some college boy dressed up for a formal date than a young conductor making his debut in one of the world's greatest opera houses, and with one of the world's mightiest music dramas. As the evening progressed, the audience was made increasingly aware that, young though he was, this conductor had both the music in his head and the performers in the palm of his hand. There were musicianship and authority in operation here; there were in his reading of this complex score a coherent conception and a high integrity. "He was apparently without self-consciousness," reported Lawrence Gilman the following morning in the *Herald Tri-*

bune, "wholly concerned with the music. It was impossible to doubt that his ability was extraordinary, that he has a musical feeling, taste, authority. He accomplished a vital, lucid, admirably rhythmed performance of the score—a performance remarkable for power, intensity, and dramatic impulse. He is . . . an artist whom one must admire and—better yet— respect."

Before that season ended, Leinsdorf conducted ten performances of *The Valkyries*, Wagner's *Parsifal*, and Richard Strauss's *Elektra*. He took on *Parsifal* (one of the longest and most exacting works in the operatic repertory) on twelve hours' notice, a performance which Lawrence Gilman described as "one of the finest that has ever been heard at the Metropolitan." The following season he led other operas, as well, including Wagner's *The Rhinegold*, *Lohengrin*, and *Tannhäuser*. All this was done in his position as second-in-command to Artur Bodanzky. Then, when Bodanzky fell seriously ill, the burden of preparing the entire German repertory for the 1939–40 season fell squarely on Leinsdorf's shoulders. He was ready, for he had long since committed to memory all these works and had carefully worked out for himself his individual ideas of their interpretation. Leinsdorf revealed such a masterful command of the music and fulfilled his duties with such extraordinary self-assurance that when Bodanzky died on November 23, 1939 (four days before the opening of the new Metropolitan Opera season), Leinsdorf was chosen as principal conductor of German opera, one of the most exacting assignments in the entire field of conducting. And he was not yet twenty-nine years old at the time!

His first year found him officiating at fifty-five performances, a truly monumental achievement. There was no decline of artistic standards at the Metropolitan. This by itself speaks volumes for the powers of a young director who overnight inherited this formidable conducting post. On the other hand, the performances had greater freshness, an increased vitality, and a more scrupulous attention to detail than they had known under Bodanzky during his last years.

That first year as principal conductor of German opera at the Metropolitan imposed colossal burdens which might have crushed and destroyed many a more experienced conductor. Not only was he responsible for all the rehearsals and performances of the Wagnerian repertory which, at that time (due to the popularity of Kirsten Flagstad, the distinguished Wagnerian soprano) dominated the season's activities. He was also compelled to study and prepare several scores he had never before conducted. During that first year he added to his repertory Wagner's *The Mastersingers, Tristan and Isolde,* and *The Twilight of the Gods;* Richard Strauss's *Der Rosenkavalier;* Debussy's *Pelleas and Melisande;* and Gluck's *Orpheus and Eurydice.* He kept working from early morning until late at night, seven days a week. Yet this was a happy time for him. He thrived on hard work and was stimulated by it. His spirits were keyed high; physically he remained in the pink of condition. At the end of the strenuous year he laughed at the suggestion that he might be in need of a vacation. "You know," was his answer, "a cocktail party exhausts me far more than a rehearsal." And instead of taking a vacation he hurled himself into the study of several new opera scores.

Leinsdorf stayed on at the Metropolitan Opera until 1943. Those were not always happy years for him, or years of complete artistic fulfillment, even though these were the years in which he grew into full maturity as a conductor of opera. The atmosphere of rivalries, petty jealousies, and dissensions which almost inevitably surrounds adulated tenors and pampered prima donnas oppressed him. On several occasions, and in spite of himself, he had been drawn helplessly into, and became personally involved in, some of these petty controversies. Besides, he was continually coming to grips with leading singers over matters of tempo or interpretation, about which he was intransigeant when he was convinced he was right. Some of the stars of the Metropolitan Opera considered him too cocksure in his opinions and ideas, too high-handed in his methods, and they openly resented him. There was, therefore, continual friction between conductor and singers. Beyond all such considerations was the fact that Leinsdorf soon began to feel that performing pretty much the same repertory year after year had a stultifying effect on him. He needed a greater horizon, greater scope, for his artistic expression.

In 1943, the Cleveland Orchestra offered him the post of musical director. He wanted a change of scene badly, but most of all he wanted a radical change of repertory. The post in Cleveland meant for him a change of pace from opera to symphonic music. It was quite true that up to that time Leinsdorf had given a number of impressive symphonic performances during guest appearances with various orchestras. But to serve as musical director of a major orchestra, and to undertake the rigors of a full season of symphony concerts, opened for Leinsdorf new areas for musical cultivation. Such a job represented a formidable test for a young musician—in fact, for the youngest musician up to that time to become musical director of a major American orchestra. But Leinsdorf knew that he had to meet this test if he was not to stunt his artistic development.

But as it turned out Cleveland was not destined to be his proving ground as a symphony conductor. Even before his first season got into high gear he was inducted into the United States Army. It was the time of World War II, and he had been a naturalized American citizen since 1942. He remained eight months in uniform. Then, with an honorable discharge on medical grounds, he could resume his career, but apparently not in Cleveland. For reasons never adequately explained, after shedding his uniform, he went back to work not in Cleveland but at the Metropolitan Opera.

Leinsdorf's development as a symphony conductor of first importance, however, had been delayed only temporarily. That development took place finally in Rochester, New York, where from 1947 to 1955 he served as the musical director of the Rochester Philharmonic. It was there, during those years, that a major opera conductor was transformed into a major symphony conductor. It was then and there that he began to build an enormous repertoire, including many modern works; that he learned how to communicate in music without the cooperation of singers, stage directors and the other accoutrements of an opera production. His amazing ability to learn new scores—to assimilate them so completely that when he conducted them he seemed to have been associated with this music for a lifetime—served him well. His penetrating musical insight enabled him to bring to each of his performances a fresh and creative approach.

It was by virtue of his achievements in Rochester that Leinsdorf eventually was chosen to take over the Boston Symphony. But this did not happen for a number of years. Between 1955 and 1961 Leinsdorf returned mainly to opera: at the New York City Opera where in 1956 he served as musical director and where for the most part he conducted a modern repertory; and from 1957 to 1962 back again at the Metropolitan Opera where he was both conductor and music consultant. However close opera was to his heart, he was eager to get back into the symphonic fold, for its vast and varied literature meant for him a kind of fulfillment he was never able to realize in opera. As he later told a Boston interviewer: "I think every conductor who has had European training wishes to do opera and symphony because this is the way we were trained. But I have had a good fill of opera; I have known the shortcomings of opera and the lovely sensations of opera. I would say that at this moment my nostalgia for opera is well controlled."

During the years between 1955 and 1961 he made a number of guest appearances with major symphony orchestras in the United States and Europe. One of these was with the Boston Symphony in February 1961, several months before this orchestra became his. He will perhaps never forget the time he rehearsed the Boston Symphony for the first time. The day was Tuesday; the date, January 31, 1961. "From my first second on the stage," he has remarked, "I was at home."

Home for Erich Leinsdorf is now in Brookline, Massachusetts, where his large, rambling, comfortable house is spacious enough to accommodate him, his wife Anne (whom he married in New York on August 3, 1939), and their five children. Through the years, Leinsdorf has learned to soften those scabrous Teutonic edges to his personality which once irritated so many. He has acquired social grace, has learned to enjoy associating with the people around him. In this respect he differs from his immediate predecessor in Boston, Charles Munch. One Bostonian put it this way: "Munch is a benign, convivial, and charming man, but he doesn't enjoy going in with a group of strangers, and he's not really comfortable unless he's speaking French. Leinsdorf, on the other hand, likes to talk, discuss, argue, listen."

Leinsdorf is short, stocky and compactly built. In *Esquire*, Milton Mayer described him as "aggressively bald between ear flaps of black hair; long face, large ears, huge hands. He still speaks with an accent, and his conversation is spiced with some of the choicest wit heard from a conductor since the days of Sir Thomas Beecham; like Beecham's his wit is often coated with acid."

Leinsdorf used to be an avid bridge player but he has long since outgrown the game. In fact all games bore him, and he is today more interested in the more intellectual pursuits of reading, introspection, and the provocative exchange of ideas. However, he also likes to collect stamps and rare vintages, he is an amateur photographer, and he is more than passingly interested in his wardrobe; as a matter of fact he is one of the best-groomed conductors in the business. He has a tolerant attitude toward rock 'n' roll, but that is only after he had been subjected to a rigorous brainwashing by his children.

After his final rehearsal for the opening concert of his regime as musical director of the Boston Symphony, Leinsdorf uttered the following word to his men: *"Calma!"* ("Be calm"). This admonition provides an illuminating insight into Leinsdorf of today as opposed to the Leinsdorf of yesterday. Once combustible, defiant, aggressive, uncompromising, Leinsdorf has learned the secret of remaining calm under stress. It was a lesson he had to learn before he could achieve greatness, and it is well that he has learned this lesson before he assumed the job with which that greatness seems assured.

GEORGE SZELL

[Born 1897]

THERE ARE FEW conductors in America today who are
feared more and more passionately disliked by the men of
their orchestras than George Szell. The reason for this is *not*
that he is a dictator—which he is. Many conductors are. Nor
that he works his men to fatigue—which he does. Many conductors do. Nor that he has no patience with mediocrity or
incompetence—which is so. Many conductors are similarly
impatient.

The reason is that in the discharge of his artistic duties he
seems to have dispensed completely with human considerations. He is unconcerned with his musicians as men; as far as
he is concerned they are performers exclusively. At rehearsals
when he addresses anyone but a first-desk man he almost
never refers to him by name, calling out instead to "clarinet"
or "oboe." It is almost as if he wants to point up the fact that
he regards each man not as a human being but as a musical instrument. He refuses to have any sort of social contact with
them or to permit personal exchanges. He is all business—
distant, aloof, cold as ice. He rarely dispenses praise, first
because he expects the best of them at all times, and then
because he is rarely satisfied. His tempers are explosive. His

cold, hard glance is as corrosive as his acidulous remarks. He can be insulting to a point of cruelty. Musicians will tell you he is utterly unreasonable; that he is hard as rock, through and through.

But if most of his men dislike him—and they do—they are also in awe of him. His knowledge of symphonic and operatic literature is encyclopedic, and nobody knows this better than the man who has to work with him day after day. There is very little that has been composed that he does not know thoroughly, and that his keen and analytical mind cannot bring back into focus at a second's notice. He knows the potential of every instrument of the orchestra as few conductors do and he has the ability to extract the best (and disguise the weakest) traits of each instrument. His baton technique is a precise scientific language that his men can understand quickly and unmistakably, a technique probably without parallel since the days of Fritz Reiner. He handles his orchestra with the command of a Heifetz playing a violin, or a Horowitz dominating a piano keyboard. It has frequently been said that any orchestra can play under Szell better than it is really capable of doing.

What his musicians appreciate most in Szell is his genius in seeing each musical masterwork steadily and seeing it whole. This is not merely a question of knowing all the notes and having committed to memory each and every marking on the printed page. This is a matter of having a masterwork so much a part of your being, and for so long a time, that the sum total of your own experiences have been subtly brought into play into its interpretation—and yet with adhering to the strictest commands of the printed page. This is why Szell once remarked that not until he was forty did he feel ready to conduct Mozart's G minor Symphony. The technical problems posed by this symphony can be handled by students; the artistic problems call for the deepest, richest resources of a great artist. What Szell sought in the Mozart symphony, what he seeks in each and every work he tackles, is what he has described as its "artistic truth." And this is not easily come by.

Now that Szell is at the height of his powers as a musical interpreter, with over half a century of conducting experience behind him, he was the rare gift of bringing to each composition the tempo, dynamics, shadings, nuances, balance that the composer demands. Thus Szell creates a different texture, a different sound for Mozart than he does for Wagner, and different ones for Beethoven than for Debussy. To each composer he applies a different set of values and a different technical equipment, down to essentials. In explaining why it is necessary to give some composers a lush and sensual treatment and others an austere and objective approach he has said: "I cannot pour chocolate syrup on asparagus."

His first love is the classical literature from Bach through Debussy, however different the style. He is probably the greatest living interpreter of this music. But his ability to uncover the most subtle and elusive intentions of a composer has also made him an extraordinary voice for the modern composer. In his study there hangs a framed letter which Sir William Walton, England's greatest composer, sent Szell after listening to Szell's recording of his Second Symphony. *"Words fail me!"* it reads. *"It is a quite fantastic and stupendous performance from every point of view. Firstly it is absolutely right musically speaking, and the virtuosity is quite staggering."*

What Szell seeks from his orchestra is not affection but admiration, because admiration rather than affection stimulates them to do their best work. His is not in the least interested in how they react to him personally. "Authority," he has said, "is more important than popularity." His only concern is how they respond to him as an artist. His first, last and sole concern is—music. He once remarked that a great artist must love music more than he loves himself, and this holds certainly true of Szell. Once when he was rehearsing the Berlin Philharmonic and working the musicians with a kind of mad fury, the manager remarked: "Mr. Szell, the way you're conducting this music, it's almost as if it were a matter of life and death." Szell replied firmly: "It is." He can permit nothing and nobody to stand in his way of the complete, the perfect, the total realization of a musical performance. Time and again, in his own career, he made enormous personal sacrifices rather than tolerate a lowering of artistic standards. This happened at the Glyndebourne Festival in England in 1947, and it happened again at the Metropolitan Opera in 1954. In each instance Szell did not hesitate to give up an important post, and in each instance he had no other place to go to. "I always let my devout consecration to music dictate my behavior," he has explained. This devout consecration to the highest standards in music has always impelled him to act the way he does toward the men of his orchestra.

Just as he feels a strong responsibility to the past by playing music the way the masters wrote it, so Szell is conscious of his duties to the present and the future. He plays a good deal of new music because he insists the modern composer must be heard and encouraged. He is also interested in developing young conductors. In his very first year in Cleveland he instituted a system of apprentice conductors which since then he has pursued assiduously. Financed by the Kolas Foundation, these young men assist in the preparation of performances. Meanwhile they study, grow and develop under Szell's penetrating guidance. For a long time Szell also spent one week a year in a workshop for young conductors set up by the Ford Foundation at the Peabody Conservatory in Baltimore.

He does what he has to do with reticence, lack of ostentation and complete indifference to publicity values. This same kind of reticence characterizes his behavior on the stage. He is singularly undemonstrative with the baton, utilizing only those gestures which are essential to carry out his commands. His baton technique is entirely functional, the last word in economy of motion. He uses a special baton which he files down with a knife and sandpapers until it is as thin and as pointed as he can possibly make it—weighing less than a quarter of an ounce and delicately balanced so that it never becomes topheavy in his fingers.

In the music he conducts, it is the architecture, the tonal design, the composer's thought patterns that are of first importance to him rather than dramatic effects or hyperthyroid outbursts. Most of the pleasure audiences get from Szell's performances springs from the inexorable logic of the music itself rather than from colors, theatrical impulses, and dramatic contrasts which so many other conductors like to superimpose on a piece of music. Szell's performances are dull only to those who require superficial trimmings to their music. But to those to whom the music itself provides complete stimulation and aesthetic satisfaction—the music unfolding with precision, transparency, and faithful adherence to a composer's intentions—Szell's performance provides as rewarding an experience as a music lover is likely to encounter in today's concert auditorium.

Under Szell, the Cleveland Orchestra, which he has now conducted for over two decades, has become one of the world's greatest; in fact there are some discriminating musicians and critics who insist that today it is *the* leading orchestra in America, if not in the world. It has become a flawless instrument, sensitively responsive to the conductor's slightest gesture, with a technical perfection second to none. These facts became more apparent to Europe than ever before when this orchestra toured in the spring of 1965 under Szell. Everywhere it performed the orchestra met with the wildest enthusiasm and excitement. This writer was in Vienna when the Cleveland Orchestra performed there for the first time. With his characteristic bravado, Szell featured on his program Schubert's C major Symphony and Haydn's Symphony No. 88 in G major, two compositions which Vienna regarded as their own and whose performances by a foreign organization Vienna would be inclined to regard with condescension if not outright hostility. The Viennese audience listened and was swept off its feet. After the concert, orchestra and conductor received a thunderous ovation that lasted some twenty minutes. At least two of Vienna's leading critics did not hesitate to place the Cleveland Orchestra above and beyond the capabilities of their own beloved Vienna Philharmonic; and all the critics were unanimous in hailing Szell as a supreme interpreter of classic German and Austrian musical literature.

To everyday living, Szell carries over the same kind of precision, sense of order, discipline, penetrating intellectual processes and fastidious attention to detail that characterize his making of music. He is extremely methodical. He arises each morning at precisely the same early hour, and everyday he goes to bed early at night at about the same hour. Four times a week he drives the two-and-a-half miles from his spacious two-story house in the Shakers Hill section of Cleveland to Severance Hall (home of the Cleveland Orchestra); you can probably set your watch by the hour and minute he leaves home each morning. He always drives his car at the same cautious speed; each year his car registers the same mileage (about three thousand miles). He is at his office by nine in the morning to clear up some correspondence before his rehearsals start at ten. Several hours later he drives back home for lunch. Since he is a gourmet he eats his meals slowly and appreciatively, each course supplemented by the appropriate wine. After lunch, on Wednesdays, he drives back to Severance Hall for an afternoon rehearsal, and then to snoop around the box office to find out about ticket sales.

Thursday and Saturday are the concert nights in Cleveland. Those days Szell partakes of a simple lunch, naps for a few hours, then dresses and takes a warm bath. Since any kind of distraction upsets him before a concert, the house is kept deathly still with visitors or telephone calls strictly ostracized. To keep his mind from worrying about the music he is directing that evening, Szell often pores into some new orchestral score while waiting for the time when he must leave for the concert hall. After the concert, the evening's music keeps running through his head and he is tormented by the places where he feels he could have done better. Since he is highly keyed emotionally, he prefers to go home with his wife after a concert, rather than attend a social function, and unwind by going mentally through his entire program.

Each year he spends four and a half months in Cleveland, four and a half months in Europe, and the rest of the time in New York. In New York he maintains a year-round apartment on Park Avenue. When in Europe he likes to return to the same hotel year after year, and whenever possible, to the same suite. One month a year in Europe is given over to complete rest and relaxation. During this period music and musicians must give way to golf (which he says he plays "gladly but badly"), omniverous reading, going to art museums, playing bridge, walking, and just resting. Coming to places with high altitudes he always spends his first twenty-four hours in bed, and the next twenty-four hours in complete relaxation, in order to get used to the rarefied atmosphere.

He has an extraordinary knowledge of painting, literature, history; and he is also remarkably well informed about politics and philosophy. He speaks half a dozen languages fluently—English, Italian, French, German, Dutch, Czech—and he has a smattering of several other tongues. First, last, and foremost he is an intellectual—an intellectual and a teacher. He is always telling golfers what's wrong with their form; professional racing drivers how to handle their cars better; tailors how to cut his clothes and couturiers how to improve the style of his wife's dresses. He gives technical advice to writers, artists, chefs. Whe he visits a restaurant he is precise in his instructions to the waiter on how his dishes are to be prepared, while in his own home, when cooking is going on, he flits in and out of the kitchen to supervise. In his conversations with friends, he often springs from his chair to consult dictionaries, encyclopedias, and the Thesaurus to check on the accuracy of what is being said.

Szell was a musical prodigy who revealed phenomenal gifts at the piano and composition. In fact it is altogether likely he could have become one of the world's foremost pianists had he chosen to specialize on the keyboard. He was born in Budapest on June 7, 1897, to an upper middle-class family, his father being a successful lawyer and businessman. As an infant of three George was able to sing some thirty or so Hungarian, Slovak, French, and German folk songs. His ear was so sensitive that whenever his mother made a mistake at the piano he would angrily slap her wrist. Music study began with a local schoolmaster when George was five. A year later, the Szell family moved to Vienna where the boy startled his parents by writing down correctly, note for note, a composition he had heard played just once. This feat led the father to contact one of Vienna's most distinguished piano teachers, Richard Robert. Under Robert, Szell made such extraordinary progress that his father decided to take him out of public school and to put him in the hands of a private tutor so that he might have more time to devote to music. "I haven't seen the inside of a classroom since," Szell recalls. "I learned more at home from my tutors than I would have in school."

Szell's debut as pianist and as composer came on the same day. In 1908 the Wiener Tonkustler Orchestra under Oskar Nebdal introduced Szell's concert overture, following which the eleven-year-old prodigy performed the Mozart A major Piano Concerto. He was praised for both efforts. From Vienna he went on to Dresden to give a concert and to London for four more performances. All proved so successful that the impresarios deluged him with offers. But Szell's father wisely decided to postpone a professional career for a number of years in order to permit the boy to develop both intellectually and musically. Instead of making concert appearances, young Szell spent the next five years studying theory and composition with eminent European teachers including Max Reger and J. B. Foerster.

When he was seventeen, Szell was vactioning at the resort town of Bad Kinnigen where a Viennese orchestra was scheduled to give a performance. On concert day, the conductor of the orchestra was hurt while playing tennis. The boy was hastily recruited as a substitute. From then on Szell knew that his future lay with conducting.

One year after that Szell appeared with the Berlin Philharmonic Orchestra in the triple role of conductor, pianist, and composer. Richard Strauss was so impressed with this exhibition that he engaged Szell as coach with the Berlin Royal Opera. For two years Szell worked with singers and musicians in the preparation of operas, and on one occasion he conducted such a masterful rehearsal of Richard Strauss's opera *Ariadne auf Naxos* that some of the men in the orchestra appealed to the opera-house director to appoint Szell as a full-time conductor. But Strauss had other plans for him. Strauss used his influence to get Szell a full-time job as principal conductor of the Strasbourg Opera where he could get richer and more varied experiences than he possibly could in Berlin.

Szell came to Strasbourg on a five-year contract but he stayed only two years. During World War I, when the French troops occupied the city, they closed down the German opera house. For a number of years Szell drifted about Europe, now playing the piano, now conducting, now composing. One of his compositions—*Variations on an Original Theme*—appeared on the programs of several major orchestras. Then, in 1924, he settled down comfortably in an all-important assignment, as chief conductor of the Berlin State Opera and the Berlin Radio Orchestra. It was in these two posts that his remarkable musical intelligence, scholarship, and conducting abilities became recognized.

After a four-week visit to the United States in 1929 to conduct several concerts in St. Louis, Szell was appointed first conductor of the German Opera in Prague. Although he soon became one of the most highly esteemed musicians in that city, and although he was given every opportunity and facility to produce the best that was in him, he was finally compelled to leave. Nazism was spreading over Central Europe and its dark shadow was hovering over Czechoslovakia. In 1937, Szell became the conductor of the Scottish Orchestra in Glasgow and the Hague Philharmonic Orchestra in Holland, dividing his musical year between these two assignments. Then when war erupted in Europe, Szell came to the United States. He was without money, job, or friends—just one more recruit in the swelling army of displaced European musicians.

For about two years Szell accepted any assignment he could find. He taught composition at the Mannes School of Music; he directed an opera workshop at the New School for Social Research; he made orchestral transcriptions for a publisher; he played the piano; on one or two occasions he conducted summer concerts. Finally, in 1941, Toscanini invited him to give a guest performance with the NBC Symphony Orchestra over the radio network. This was the showcase Szell needed to prove himself to Americans, and he proved it with a stunning concert. On the strength of this single appearance, Szell was swamped with offers for guest appearances with leading American symphonic organizations; he was also engaged as a principal conductor of German operas at the Metropolitan Opera in New York.

Szell stayed three years at the Metropolitan. His performances of the Wagner *Ring* cycle, Wagner's *The Mastersingers* and *Tannhäuser*, Mozart's *Don Giovanni*, and Richard Strauss's *Salome* and *Der Rosenkavalier* inspired ovations from audiences and accolades from critics. Here is what Virgil Thomson said in the *Herald Tribune* when Szell made his Metropolitan Opera debut on December 9, 1942, with *Salome*: "The occasion was enhanced by the debut . . . of the celebrated Czech conductor, George Szell, who directed the work with power, precision, and all imaginable exactitude of expression. Last night's revival . . . was orchestrally and vocally superb. . . . The performance was a rich and grand one; and the major credit must go, of course, to Mr. Szell. The score was squeezed for every effect and yet the great line of it was kept intact and the sonorities remained within the domain of 'legitimate' musical sounds. Mr. Szell did a virtuoso job on a difficult and complex work. . . . He made all the music sound and sound well."

In 1946 the directors of the Cleveland Orchestra were on the look-out for a new music director—its last one, Artur Rodzinski, having withdrawn in 1943. After scouring the country, the Musical Arts Association (which controlled the destinies of the Cleveland Orchestra) decided on Szell. Szell agreed to come—but only on the condition that the Association stood ready and willing to place all decisions on artistic policy in his hands. "I must be the absolute master," he told the Association firmly, "and if I am, I can promise you that in time the Cleveland Orchestra will have no superiors anywhere in the world."

His conditions met, Szell came to Cleveland, rolled up his sleeves and went to work. Of the ninety-four musicians, twelve were dismissed, and before the first season ended ten others resigned rather than submit to Szell's withering criticisms, badgering, abuse, and military discipline. This building-up process continued the next season, and the season after that. Whenever an outstanding orchestral musician became available anywhere, he was lured to Cleveland with an attractive contract. In a few years' time only thirty-five men were left from the orchestra Rodzinski had conducted. The others —and the orchestral complement had been increased from ninety-four to one hundred and six men—were the best that money could buy. Even so, these consummate musicians had to be subjected to the most grueling drilling until one hundred and six men responded to Szell as one man. "*We* begin to rehearse," Szell has said proudly, "when other orchestras are finished."

Other changes, besides those in personnel, were instituted, always leading toward growth and expansion. A twenty-week season was extended to forty-eight weeks, with the orchestra now giving about 150 concerts. The number of educational concerts swelled to fifty-five a year, reaching one hundred thousand children. A two hundred and forty voice chorus was established under the brilliant leadership of Robert Shaw, one of America's ablest choral directors; it collaborated with the orchestra in the presentation of choral masterworks. The system of hiring apprentice conductors was, as we have already had occasion to note, initiated. Extensive tours were realized for the first time in the orchestra's history: Europe in 1957; the first transcontinental tour of the United States in 1960; Europe, the Soviet Union and countries behind the Iron Curtain in 1965 under the auspices of the Department of State. In addition to all this, almost a quarter of a million dollars was spent at Szell's insistence to improve the acoustics of Severance Hall.

In time, Szell made the orchestra in his own image—the way Toscanini once had done with the New York Philharmonic and Leopold Stokowski with the Philadelphia Orchestra. "Cleveland is my home," he will now tell you, "and the Cleveland Orchestra is my orchestra." It *is* Szell's orchestra as more than one critic at home and abroad have written. Paul Hume, the distinguished music critic of the Washington *Post*, put it this way: "The Cleveland Orchestra today is wholly Szell's creation. Its members may pride themselves in being able to do anything he asks of them, for there is no finer accomplishment open to them in their profession. It is with their gifts, their technique, their tone, and above all their ability to respond to his musical intellect that Szell has fashioned them into one of the magnificent symphonic ensembles of our time. It is out of his mind and heart that the music flows in a way that no other conductor and orchestra in this country today produces it."

LEONARD BERNSTEIN

[Born 1918]

THERE IS HARDLY a facet of our musical life that has not been touched and enriched by Leonard Bernstein's genius. He is a composer, both serious and popular. His music is performed the world over on symphony programs, and it is heard on Broadway and in motion pictures; it has even been represented on best-selling lists of "pop" recordings.

He is the nation's music teacher. For many years he was in charge of a class of conducting at the Berkshire Music Centre in Tanglewood, Massachusetts, and for much longer than that he has explained the mysteries of great music and musical performances over television to both young and old. He has even converted the Thursday evening subscription series of the New York Philharmonic Orchestra into "previews" so that he might tell his audiences something about the music they are going to hear.

In addition, he is a concert pianist; the author of two best-selling books on music appreciation as well as of articles on music for leading periodicals; and he is the indefatigable crusader for the new and the original in modern music.

But perhaps most of all, he is a conductor, now one of the world's greatest, who has everywhere inspired the kind of adulation, and generated the kind of excitement, Toscanini used to create in his heyday. In fact not since Toscanini has there appeared a conductor whose biography so reads like legend as Bernstein's.

Bernstein's phenomenal versatility is in its own right the kind of stuff out of which legends are made. But his achievements appear even more incredible when we remember that he has not only been a major success in every muscial endeavor he has undertaken, but he has become so with his first try. The first orchestral work he ever wrote, the *Jeremiah Symphony*, was forthwith performed by America's leading orchestras, was recorded by RCA Victor, and received the New York Music Critics Circle Award. The first ballet score he ever wrote was for *Fancy Free* which, from its première on, became one of the leading contributions to the contemporary dance repertory. His first musical comedy was *On the Town*, which ran on Broadway for over a year, was made into a successful movie starring Frank Sinatra and Gene Kelly, and subsequently had two off-Broadway revivals. His first book, *The Joy of Music*, was a national best seller.

And the first time he ever conducted a professional orchestra, he led one of the greatest of them all, the New York Philharmonic; and with that single performance he became a conducting celebrity.

Not since Toscanini has there been a conducting debut to equal that of Bernstein in high tension, drama, and performance achievement. The parallel between these two debuts—those of Toscanini and Bernstein—is so striking that perhaps it might be wise here and now to recall briefly how the Maestro (the greatest conductor of the twentieth century) made his bow. Toscanini was nineteen, a cellist in the orchestra of a traveling opera company, when he arrived in Rio de

Janeiro for a performance of Verdi's *Aida*. Because the company's regular music director had a falling out with the manager, *Aida* found itself without a conductor. Although young Toscanini had never conducted a performance of any kind in his life, he was recruited to take over the baton, because he was known for his fabulous memory, ear, and musicianship. Toscanini came to the conductor's stand and, without the benefit of a single rehearsal, gave an electrifying performance of *Aida* such as Rio de Janeiro had never before heard; and what is even more astonishing, he conducted the whole performance from memory.

This incredible story, true in every detail, was almost duplicated to the letter when Leonard Bernstein made his first public appearance at the head of a major orchestra. The date was November 14, 1943, a Sunday afternoon; the place, Carnegie Hall. Bernstein, aged twenty-five, was then in his first season as assistant conductor to Artur Rodzinski of the New York Philharmonic, a job which entailed helping out at rehearsals.

The world-famous Bruno Walter was scheduled to appear as guest conductor of the New York Philharmonic that Sunday afternoon. But late the preceding Saturday, while attending a party, Bernstein received a telephone call from Bruno Zirato, manager of the Philharmonic. Bruno Walter, he said, had fallen ill and would not be able to perform, and nobody had yet been found available to take his place. Did Bernstein feel he could step in as a substitute? Zirato pointed out to Bernstein that this would mean that Bernstein was making his official debut without a rehearsal; but Zirato also pointed out that if anybody could accomplish this, Bernstein could. Bernstein's reply was that if he was needed he would be ready.

Although the hour was late, Bernstein rushed back to his

studio to look over the music scheduled for the program the following day. One of the compositions was a world première —Miklos Rozsa's *Theme and Variations*. The other numbers were familiar masterworks, but of the kind of tax the capacities of an even experienced conductor: Schumann's *Manfred Overture;* Richard Strauss's *Don Quixote;* Wagner's Prelude to *The Mastersingers.* "I stayed up until 4:30 a.m., alternately dozing, sipping coffee, and studying scores," Bernstein later recalled. "I fell into a sound sleep about 5:30 A.M. and awakened at 9 A.M. An hour later Mr. Zirato telephoned and said, 'You're going to conduct.' My first reaction was one of shock. I then became excited over my unexpected debut and, I may add, not a little frightened. Knowing it would be impossible to assemble the orchestra for a rehearsal on Sunday, I went over to Mr. Walter's home and went over the scores with him. I found Mr. Walter sitting up but wrapped in blankets, and he obligingly showed me just how he did it."

At three o'clock that afternoon Bruno Zirato came to the stage of Carnegie Hall to announce that, since Bruno Walter was sick in bed, a substitute would take over. "You are going to witness the debut of a full-fledged conductor, born, educated, and trained in this country," he told the audience. Then Bernstein came forward with bold and vigorous strides. He looked more like a college undergraduate than a Maestro. His youth was pointed up by the business suit he was wearing; he did not own formal attire. Then without further ado, he gave the downbeat for the opening chords of Schumann's *Manfred Overture.* It did not take long for the audience in Carnegie Hall—and the unseen audience around the country who were listening in on the coast-to-coast broadcast—that a great conductor was being born that day. After the concert ended, eight crews of photographers, hastily summoned from all over the city, began to take pictures of Bernstein. The next day both *The New York Times* and the *Herald Tribune* carried the story of the debut on the front page, as an event of first importance. *The New York Times* even devoted an editorial to this performance. Olin Downes, that newspaper's music critic, remarked prophetically that Bernstein "shows that he is one of the very few conductors of the rising generation who are indubitably to be reckoned with. . . . It was clear at once that . . . he was conducting the orchestra in his own right, and not the orchestra conducting him; that he had every one of the scores both in his hands and in his head; and though he logically and inevitably conformed in broad outline, he was not following slavishly in the footsteps of his distinguished senior. Mr. Bernstein thought for himself and obtained his wishes." The critic of the *Daily News* reached out to baseball for an analogue to point up Bernstein's success. He said: "Like a shoestring catch in the centerfield—make it and you're a hero. Muff it and you're a dope. Bernstein made it."

Where do you go when you *start* at the top? The only direction is downwards. But Leonard Bernstein defied the laws of gravity. He started at the top and from that point went on into the stratosphere. The composer of the *Jeremiah Symphony* has written works like *The Age of Anxiety*, the *Kaddish*, and the *Chichester Psalms* which have placed him solidly with the foremost serious American composer of our times. The writer of *On the Town* has written scores for such resounding Broadway successes as *Wonderful Town* (which starred Rosalind Russell on Broadway for two seasons) and the epoch-making *West Side Story*, which opened new horizons for both the musical theater and motion pictures. The nation's music teacher over the television has won more top awards

93

than any musician, serious or popular, including the two highest tributes the industry could bestow on him, the Sylvania and George Foster Peabody Awards. And the conductor who stepped into Bruno Walter's shoes to make his debut became, in 1958, one of the youngest men, and the only one of American birth, ever to become music director of the New York Philharmonic Orchestra. More than that—with appearances with virtually every major orchestra in the world, and in some of the world's greatest opera houses (including La Scala, the Metropolitan Opera, and the Vienna State Opera) he went on to become one of the most sought-after conductors in the world, one of the few always calculated to tax the capacity of any auditorium, and to arouse in audiences the most excited responses.

He was born to make music; but most of all he was born to be a conductor. His physical birth took place in Lawrence, Massachusetts, on August 25, 1918. His musical one followed when an aunt sent over an old weatherbeaten upright piano to the Bernstein household. He was eleven years old at the time and as he later recalled "I made love to it right away." From that moment on, as soon as he came home from school, he would rush to the piano and stay there for hours. He picked out the tunes of familiar melodies (mostly the popular hits of the day) for which he would improvise accompaniments. Late one night his fumblings at the piano were disturbing the family in its sleep. The father upbraided him: "Lenny, don't you know it's two o'clock?" Lenny replied: "I know. But the sounds are in my head and I just have to get them out."

All this preoccupation with music did not sit well with Leonard's father, who conducted a successful business supplying beauty parlors and barber shops. The father had every intention of having Leonard come into his business some day;

94

besides he was in horror of a profession like music that seemed to promise only struggle and starvation except to an elect few. He tried to coax Leonard from the piano, tried to get him interested in other pursuits. But to no avail. "I knew with finality," Bernstein says, "I would be a musician."

He went out and found a piano teacher whose fee was one dollar a lesson which he paid out of his pocket money. That teacher did not satisfy him, so he sought out a second who was even worse. Finally, he found a remarkable teacher in Helen Coates, under whose sensitive guidance and encouragement he grew, developed, and flourished. "He was frighteningly gifted," Helen Coates later told an interviewer. "He could read, sing, and memorize anything. He absorbed in one lesson an arrangement that took most of my pupils five or six lessons to learn." Helen Coates urged Bernstein to go to the library and borrow the scores of symphonies and operas which she would then discuss with him. She encouraged him to try his hand at composing. One day he brought her a piano concerto he had written under the influence of Tchaikovsky. She advised him to go to the concerts of the Boston Symphony and to keep an ear alert for new music. Before very long he discovered the world of Stravinsky and Prokofiev.

It was music all the time for Lenny. "I didn't exist without music," he says. Nevertheless, he also did exceedingly well at school. In 1935 he was graduated from the Boston Latin School with honors, in the top ten percent of his class. The next stop was Harvard, as preparation for a successful career in business thought Father Bernstein. But Leonard felt that Harvard was just a way of marking time before he would be able to devote himself entirely and exclusively to music.

He stayed at Harvard the full four years, graduating with a Bachelor of Arts degree in 1939. He was a consistently good student in most subjects, and brilliant in a few (languages and philosophy, for example). In music he was one of a kind. At Harvard he studied counterpoint, theory, and music history with Walter Piston and Edward Burlingame Hill among others. Outside Harvard, he continued piano study with one of Boston's most distinguished teachers, Heinrich Gebhard, who fed him a healthy diet of twentieth-century music. Where there was music at Harvard, there was Bernstein; and when he was there making music, it was of the highest order. He served as piano accompanist for the Harvard Glee Club. He wrote music for and performed in college-day japes. He played the piano for presentations of silent motion-picture classics, creating his own background music. Irving Fine, himself a distinguished American composer and Bernstein's fellow-student at Harvard in the late 1930s, recalled: "I remember with great nostalgia his appearance as piano accompanist at a series of historical films presented by the Harvard Film Society. The Battleship Potemkin rode at anchor to the accompaniment of Copland's Piano Variations, excerpts from Stravinsky's *Petrouchka*, and Bernstein's own paraphrases of Russian folk songs." Bernstein also performed at concerts of the Harvard Music Club, often recruited at the last moment to substitute for an artist unable to make an appearance. "Many programs," added Fine, "would have been lost if Bernstein had not been willing to tackle, almost at sight, anything from the Stravinsky Concerto for Two Solo Pianos to a work by one of his fellow students. At these club meetings he performed some of his own earliest essays."

In his last year at Harvard, Bernstein wrote the music for a production of Aristophanes' *The Birds* presented by the Harvard Classical Club. This Greek drama, with Bernstein's music, was given at Cambridge on April 21, 1939. What is particularly important about this performance is that Bernstein conducted for the first time in his life. An even more ambitious attempt at conducting came soon after that when Bernstein led a performance at Cambridge of Marc Blitzstein's social-conscious opera, *The Cradle Will Rock*. These two attempts at directing musical performances whetted his appetite. But his first conscious ambition to become a conductor became crystallized at Harvard when he was introduced to the world-famous conductor, Dimitri Mitropoulos. A warm friendship developed between them. Mitropoulos began referring to Bernstein playfully as "the genius boy." He was the first one to advise Bernstein to think seriously of a career as conductor.

Meanwhile, Bernstein's father still hoped that when the boy graduated from Harvard he would enter the family business; in fact he later told an interviewer he insisted that Leonard do so. "From the early sixteenth century my family never made a livelihood in art," he explained, "and I didn't want to break this tradition. I also felt Lenny could make a better living in business. Remember there was no Leonard Bernstein then. There might not be another Leonard Bernstein for a thousand years. I'm very proud of Lenny but . . . because God blessed the world with a Leonard Bernstein, it doesn't mean his parents should expect it. You don't *expect* your son to be a Moses, a Maimonides, a Leonard Bernstein. If I had to do it a over again, I'd do the same thing."

Unable to win his father over to his own way of thinking, Leonard decided to leave him, to come to New York, and to start looking around for ways and means of earning his living through music. He did not have an easy time. He could not get any employment as pianist because he was not a member of the Musicians' Union; the Union required a six-month period of residence in New York before membership was granted. Other musical jobs were few and far between. "There was just no place for me," he says of this depressing period. But with the help of Mitropoulos, Leonard managed to get a scholarship for the Curtis Institute of Music in Philadelphia to study conducting with Fritz Reiner, and he continued his piano training with Isabelle Vengerova. Bernstein stayed at the Curtis Institute from the fall of 1939 until June 1941. He performed whatever problem or exercise Reiner set before him with such aplomb, infallible instinct, and a command of technique that Reiner came to call him "the most talented, all-around student I ever had."

From the Curtis Institute, Bernstein went on to the Berkshire Music Center at Tanglewood, in Lenox, Massachusetts, as a scholarship student in conducting. Bernstein became Serge Koussevitzky's pupil and protégé. Even then Koussevitzky saw in the young Bernstein a possible successor to himself at the head of the Boston Symphony. It was for this reason that, one day, he urged Leonard Bernstein to change his name for a European one that might be more euphonious, and look more attractive on a program and a billboard. "The conductor of the Boston Symphony," Koussevitzky told him firmly, "will never be somebody who is called Leonard Bernstein!" Bernstein replied just as firmly that if he was ever to achieve a successful career as conductor it would have to be with the name with which he was born. Adopting a phony name for the sake of buying success was an act of dishonesty Bernstein would not consider.

In the summer of 1943, Bernstein received a message at Tanglewood that Artur Rodzinski, then the newly appointed musical director of the New York Philharmonic Orchestra, wanted to see him at his farm in nearby Stockbridge. "How would you like to be my assistant conductor next season?" Rodzinski asked Bernstein when he arrived. Rodzinski had heard Bernstein conduct several student performances at Tanglewood and had been impressed. Bernstein was taken aback by Rodzinski's offer. He had never conducted a professional orchestra in his life, and here he was being offered a job as assistant conductor to one of the world's greatest symphonic institutions!

Things began moving quickly for Bernstein after that. He assumed the assistant conductor's post in the fall of 1943. Only a few weeks after he had helped out with the first rehearsal he was pushed by Fate into the limelight when he had to substitute for Bruno Walter at a Sunday afternoon concert. Unknown on November 14, 1943, Leonard Bernstein awoke on the morning of November 15 to discover he was a national celebrity.

His career advanced with giant steps after that. His highly publicized debut with the New York Philharmonic brought him guest engagements with seven important American orchestras, including the Boston Symphony. In 1945, he had an orchestra of his own, the New York City Symphony, which he led for three seasons. In May 1946 he was the main attraction at a music festival in Prague, and in 1947 he made a triumphant tour of Europe and Palestine. Meanwhile, in 1944, he had also won accolades as a serious composer (with the *Jeremiah Symphony*), as a composer of ballet music (with *Fancy Free*), as a composer of musical comedies (with *On the Town*). One year after his momentous New York Philharmonic debut he was one of the most publicized musicians in America, if not in the world, a "triple-note man of music," as *The New York Times* then described him. His photograph appeared on the covers of national-circulation magazines.

99

Bobby soxers mobbed him in the street for his autograph. The United States Chamber of Commerce named him the outstanding young man of 1944.

Success followed success in a seemingly endless procession. At La Scala, Milan, he became the first American-born conductor to lead performances in that historic opera house; this took place in 1953. In 1954, when he made his first appearance on television in a discussion of Beethoven's Fifth Symphony, he opened altogether new vistas for music apprecation and music education—before an audience in the millions. In Tel Aviv, in 1957, he was the conductor selected to open the new concert hall, the Frederick R. Mann Auditorium, with the proper pomp and ceremony. In 1958 he was the first American ever appointed as music director of the New York Philharmonic. In that same year he took the Philharmonic on a historic 15,000 mile tour of South and Central America where he conducted thirty-nine concerts in twenty-one cities of twelve different countries. In 1959 he made an even more epoch-making tour with his orchestra, this time to Europe, the Near East, the Soviet Union and other countries behind the Iron Curtain, now giving fifty performances in twenty-nine cities of seventeen countries. And in 1962 he ushered in a new era of American music when he helped open Philharmonic Hall at Lincoln Center in New York with a festive concert with the New York Philharmonic Orchestra (which was also beamed around the country and in Canada over television).

There is hardly a place in the civilized world where he has not aroused the most extravagant enthusiasm. He is undoubtedly one of the greatest—possibly *the* greatest—box-office attraction among living conductors.

Why was his success so immediate, so universal; and why has it remained so endurable?

One reason lies in the fantastic way in which, from his very beginnings, he was able to adapt himself to the art and science of conducting. He can master even the most complex score with a single reading. He has the gift of penetrating to the heart and core of every piece of music he studies. He knows how to impress his ideas and intentions on his musicians.

Another reason lies in his exciting personality that discharges sparks the moment he appears on the stage to ignite the enthusiasm of both performers and audiences. His extravagant gestures, which have tempted one writer to call him a ballet dancer, galvanize the musicians in front of him into excitingly dramatic performances.

There is still a further reason, and that one lies in his youth. In a calling dominated by middle-aged, even old men, he has, without sacrificing the quality of musical presentation, introduced the brashness, enthusiasm, forthrightness, courage, honesty, and overbrimming energy of youth. He is youth in the way he has become the spokesman for young composers and performers, mostly Americans; in the way he has fought the battle for the most advanced tendencies in music and found an important place for them on his programs. He is youth in the way he always speaks his mind on every important issue without considering expediency or tact. He is youth in the way he gets excited over what he is doing and in his ability to infect those who listen to him with excitement, whether he is performing on the piano, conducting an orchestra, or lecturing. And while his youth is now behind him and he is now in his middle years, he has somehow magically retained his infectious youthful spirit and bravado. Despite the enormous work load he carries throughout the year in the many different areas of his activity, he has never permitted physical fatigue or weariness of spirit to set in.

He is a demon for hard work because his seeming inexhaustible enthusiasm for every field of music allows him neither peace nor rest once an activity has seized him. This is why he has been so generous in scattering his energies. He is an early riser, usually at dawn. After a cup of coffee he generally uses these early hours to study one of the new scores he is conducting that week. After two hours of such study he has his breakfast (often with one or more people with whom he must discuss business affairs). The mornings are devoted to rehearsing the New York Philharmonic. Though the rehearsal taxes his physical and mental resources, his day's work really begins when the rehearsal period is over. This is the time he must have conferences with agents, managers, producers; when he must find time for interviewers and photographers; when he must talk over problems with collaborators; when he must plan and sketch out ideas for his television programs.

Dinner is the time for leisure and relaxation. If there is no concert scheduled that evening or some pressing social engagement, Bernstein can now devote himself to quiet pleasures: visits from intimate friends with whom he enjoys discussions on politics, literature, psychology, poetry, art, the theater, and all the other extra-musical interests that absorb him. Sometimes he and his friends indulge in a game of anagrams; sometimes he joins his wife in informal sessions of two-piano music; most of the time he plays with his children.

His wife is the former Felicia Montealegre, a Chilean by birth, who had come to New York to pursue a career in the theater and who eventually made a number of successful appearances on television. They were married in Boston on September 9, 1951, and have since then raised three children—Jamie, Alexander Serge (named after Koussevitzky), and Nina. The Bernsteins have two homes. One is a large duplex that occupies the two top floors of a Park Avenue apartment house, "a happy melange of antique and contemporary" as Joan Cook described it in *The New York Times,* "all but two rooms decorated by Mrs. Bernstein. . . . Guests get off the elevator at the top floor, enter a small attractively appointed foyer and move into a large hall, done in black and white, with a gracefully curved staircase that leads to the family living quarters on the floor below. The effect is one of a country house rather than an apartment, a place that abounds with flowers, plants and riotous colors." The Bernsteins also have a country home for holidays and weekends in Fairfield, Connecticut.

When he has a performance to give, Bernstein eats little and reaches Philharmonic Hall well ahead of concert time. During the intermission he is massaged with cologne, a period in which he grumbles about all the things that have thus far gone wrong and points to the places where improvement could have been made. After the concert is over he meets hordes of friends, colleagues, acquaintances in the artist's room. Then he goes off to partake of a hearty meal and often to a party somewhere.

His day, then, is rigorously systematized, with a time and place for everything that must be done. His extraordinary powers of concentration enable him to work anywhere he can find a free moment. He has sketched out ideas for compositions on trains, in taxis, at airports, in hotel lobbies. He is also able to work oblivious of distractions around him. One thing of which he is incapable is moderation. Whether in work or play he hurls himself completely into what he is doing. His wife has said: "Lenny never does anything in half measures. If we're playing anagrams, he always wants to play till dawn. If we watch the Late Show on TV he always wants to watch the Late Late Show after that. If we go to a movie, he will want to step into another movie right away. If he plays with the children, he plays long and hard."

To the often voiced criticism that he is trying to do too many things, instead of specializing, he has this reply: "It's perfectly possible to do all the things I have to do." He has also said: "An artist has the compulsion to work. He'd go crazy if he didn't. I love all my work—all of it." He simply *has* to communicate in every branch of music that fascinates him. What makes him unique is that, unlike so many other musicians, he is fascinated by every branch of music. Such is his physical and nervous make-up that he thrives on diversity. He seems to have an endless reservoir of energy and zest. He maintains a pace that would exhaust practically everybody else, and first begins to increase his momentum with a renewed burst of energy at a point where others have become vitiated. He often explains that to take on a musical job completely different from one just finished is a revitalizing force for him. "I never get tired of working," he insists.

And so he turns a deaf ear to all well-intentioned advice that he canalize his genius into a single artery. And he will probably continue to enrich the many and varied branches of music in which he has become involved for many years to come.

WILLIAM STEINBERG

[Born 1899]

WILLIAM STEINBERG's success as the musical director of the
Pittsburgh Symphony is essentially the triumph of sound musicianship and scholarship over superficial values. Steinberg
belongs to that distinguished company of European conductors (of whom Bruno Walter of the recent past was such a
noble representative) who never permit personal behavior or
idiosyncrasies to attract the limelight. Their job is to make
music on the highest possible level, and to this task they bring
not only complete dedication but also the most searching musical intelligence. Their behavior on the conductor's platform,
and their baton technique, are discreet and reserved, directed
not toward the eye of the audience but toward that of the
musicians. At performances, these conductors shun showman-
ship, just as at rehearsals they dispense with tantrums or pyro-
technical displays of artistic temperament. They do their
work quietly, efficiently, with the best possible manners, and
with the utmost of consideration for those with whom they
work. Their self-effacement springs not from undue modesty,
but from their desire to glorify composer and music.

Today Steinberg is the cream of this choice crop. In making the Pittsburgh Symphony one of the five or six greatest

orchestras in the United States he has operated unobtrusively, undemonstratively, without the accompanying fanfares of publicity bugles. He has worked long and hard to build the orchestra up to its present prestige from the lowly plateau into which it had fallen after Fritz Reiner left in 1948. Attendance was off, and so were the financial contributions. The season was shortened. For four years guest conductors came and went; since none had directorial responsibility, the orchestra languished in mediocrity. Then following his stunning success in guest appearances, William Steinberg was chosen as musical director. This was in 1952. Under Steinberg, the slow process of rehabilitation began to take place. As the quality of performance improved, so did the attendance. The season was extended, the orchestral budget was doubled. An endowment fund of five million dollars was established. Orchestra and conductor began making distinguished and successful recordings.

In less than a decade, the number of local concerts was increased from sixty-five to one hundred and twenty-four. On extended tours of the United States, the orchestra now stood ready to stand comparison with America's other noble symphonic institutions. In 1963–64, for example, the Pittsburgh Symphony gave fifty-one concerts in thirteen states, traveling about ten thousand miles in three buses. Finally it was willing to challenge Europe as well. Sponsored by the Cultural Presentations Program of the Department of State, the Pittsburgh Symphony made an eleven-week tour of fourteen European and Middle Eastern countries in 1964, covering some 25,000 miles, and appearing at leading festivals in Edinburgh, Baalbeck, Athens, and Warsaw. Coals were being carried to Newcastle (so to speak) when Steinberg led the works of German and Austrian masters during his appearances in those two countries, and compositions by Edward Elgar in concerts in England. Elsewhere, as in Warsaw, modern American composers were liberally represented. But whatever the program, and wherever the place, the response was one of extraordinary enthusiasm. A statement by the critic of Lisbon's *Diario de Manha* perhaps best sums up the European response to the performances of the Pittsburgh Symphony: "There are no restrictions to be made concerning the quality of the orchestra; it is of the highest category and its perfection is total."

No wonder, then, that music lovers in Pittsburgh are saying that William Steinberg has achieved a "musical miracle" in their city. Week after week he gives them programs solidly grounded on the firm foundations of the musical masterworks, each performance presented with such thoroughness and such attention to detail that one critic in Pittsburgh was led to remark that Steinberg gives of himself at every concert as if it were the last he was destined to give. Modern music may play somewhat less of a role in Pittsburgh than it does, say, in Boston, Philadelphia, or New York. Nevertheless, Steinberg has made notable contributions to the modern repertory by presenting the premières of several works now acknowledged to be staples in the symphonic repertory. These include Ernest Toch's Symphony No. 3 (which received the Pulitzer Prize in music in 1957) and Hindemith's *Pittsburgh Symphony* (which the composer considered one of his finest works for orchestra and which the Pittsburgh Symphony had commissioned him to write).

William Steinberg was born in Cologne, Germany, on August 1, 1899. He was a musical prodigy who early revealed remarkable capabilities on both the violin and the piano. At thirteen he conducted a performance of one of his own compositions: a setting for chorus and orchestra of a text from Ovid's *Metamorphoses*. His musical training continued for a number of years at the Cologne Conservatory. There he made such progress as a conducting pupil of Herman Abendroth that, upon his graduation in 1919, he was given the Wullner Prize. Otto Klemperer, one of Germany's eminent conductors of opera and symphonic music, was so impressed by Steinberg's conducting potential that he hired him as his assistant at the Cologne Opera. There, in 1924, Steinberg was elevated to the post of first conductor.

In 1925, Steinberg became the principal conductor of the German Opera in Prague. During the four years that he retained this post, he made a number of impressive guest appearances in Germany and Austria, including several at the renowned Berlin State Opera. By 1929 his fame was secure. One of the choice musical assignments in Europe fell in his hands when he became musical director of the city of Frankfort-on-the-Main. This job entailed the direction of both operatic and symphonic performances.

His ripening gifts as musical interpreter, which was receiving recognition all over Europe, did not spare him when, in 1933, the Nazis rose to power in Germany. Because he was a Jew, Steinberg was compelled to resign his post in Frankfort, after which he was made to leave Germany. When, in 1936, Arturo Toscanini helped to organize the Palestine Symphony Orchestra (made up mainly of refugee musicians from Germany) Steinberg became its conductor.

In 1938, Steinberg was invited by Toscanini to come to the United States. Toscanini made Steinberg his assistant with the NBC Symphony Orchestra, which was then giving concerts over the coast-to-coast radio network; some of these Steinberg conducted in Toscanini's absence. For a number of years after that Steinberg appeared as a guest conductor of major American orchestras, and in 1944 he appeared with the San Francisco Opera.

In 1945, Steinberg acquired an American orchestra of his own when he became the musical director of the Buffalo Symphony in New York. This was a minor league orchestra at the time, but it did not take Steinberg long to raise it to major-league status. That job completed, Steinberg passed on to Pittsburgh in 1952 where he was since remained. For two years he served concurrently as music director of two orchestras, the Pittsburgh Symphony and England's London Philharmonic. But the expanding program of activity in Pittsburgh finally compelled him to concentrate on that city alone and to confine his appearances elsewhere to guest performances. In 1964–65 he took sabbatical leave from the Pittsburgh Symphony in order to conduct the New York Philharmonic and at the Metropolitan Opera in New York (his first appearances in that opera house), among many other prominent symphonic and operatic organizations in America and Europe.

Steinberg lives with his wife Lotti in a ranch-type house in the Squirrel Hill section of Pittsburgh. There they have raised two children: a son, Arthur, who has become a noted archaeologist and a member of the faculty of the Massachusetts Institute of Technology; and a daughter, Sylvia, who raised a family of her own in Long Island, New York.

Steinberg's life is Pittsburgh is well ordered. Mornings are usually spent at rehearsals; afternoons are devoted to correspondence, the study of scores, a stroll through the Schenley Park district, and to a refreshing but brief nap. Before a concert he partakes of a steak, always cooked rare; and after concert time he relaxes with a cup of hot chocolate.

Bald, of medium height and unimpressive in build, Steinberg does not cut much of a dashing figure either on the platform or off it. But his face is expressive in reflecting every nuance and shade of his feelings, and his small black eyes are intense and arresting. He likes to smoke a pipe, and to drink an occasional highball. He enjoys television (particularly mystery shows) and he is an ardent movie fan. He loves paintings and is a frequent visitor to art museums. In the winter time he gets his exercise by hiking or taking leisurely walks; in the summer, by swimming.

He is continually hounded to make guest appearances with the world's great orchestras and opera companies. His taxing schedule in Pittsburgh, however, compels him to turn down over three-quarters of these offers. "My correspondence," he will tell you, "is chiefly to turn down invitations." He can, therefore, pick his spots. The one that gave him uncommon pleasure was a return to Berlin in February 1964 after many years of absence; on that occasion he was the first American to appear in West Berlin's new Philharmonic Hall. His success in Berlin was spectacular. It would have proved a most touching homecoming for a German-born musician. It was even more gratifying to William Steinberg—a German-born musician who was now an American.

JOSEPH KRIPS

[Born 1902]

J oseph krips, musical director of the San Francisco Symphony Orchestra, is a Central European conductor in the
grand tradition of Bruno Walter—an artist whose musical
performances never permit the intrusion of personal idiosyncrasies, eccentricities, or displays of temperament. At rehearsals, on the concert stage, and in his personal life Krips is the
last word in self-effacement. "I learned to be humble before
great music and great composers," he once told a interviewer.
That humility never permitted him to indulge in the kind of
terpischorean exhibitions on the dais with which so many
other conductors like to attract the interest of their audiences.
His movements of body and hands are efficient and undemonstrative. "I conduct only for the composer," he insists. His
humility would also never allow him to indulge in "interpretations"—that is, trying to increase the emotional or dramatic
impact of a composition through the imposition of his own
ideas that are in contradiction to those of the creator. What
the composer has tried to say is what Krips tries to express as
honestly and as accurately as he can.

He is not cut out to be a matinee idol. He is a big man, and
somewhat ungainly, bald, with a round and pleasant face that

has been compared to that of a kewpie doll. The attention he attracts the world over, therefore, comes not from the way he looks or behaves or from any gift at inspiring publicity stories. It comes exclusively from his musical endowments and achievements. He is today one of the greatest living interpreters of the classical and romantic literature of the German and Austrian school, opera as well as symphony. He has few rivals in the music of Mozart, Beethoven, Brahms, and Bruckner.

Like so many other distinguished conductors who have enriched our musical lives in this country for the past quarter of a century, Krips was a helpless, innocent victim of the social and political upheavals attending the rise of the Nazis in Germany and Austria in the late 1930s. He was born in Vienna on August 8, 1902, to a musical family. His father, a physician, was an amateur singer who was a member of the Karmeliter Church Choir which Joseph joined when he was only six. Although the father encouraged little Joseph to make music, he was not tolerant toward a professional career. Krips recalls: "In a career so difficult as that of the professional musician, he felt that everything should be done to prevent a child from adopting it. Then, if he still persists in spite of all obstacles, he really is fitted for it." Since Joseph persisted in making music whenever and wherever he could, the father put no obstacles in his way. At thirteen, Joseph began studying the violin, paying for the lessons out of his weekly allowance. His formal musical education took place at the Vienna Academy, which he entered when he was sixteen, and where his teachers included one of the most distinguished conductors of his generation, Felix Weingartner. It was not long before Krips got a job as violinist in the orchestra of the Volksoper which was then conducted by Weingartner. During the three years he filled this post he also served as a member of a touring opera company where he officiated, as he now recalls, as "choir conductor, stage manager, harmonium player, and at certain difficult moments, even chief of the claque."

Felix Weingartner was holding auditions at the Volksoper when the regular piano accompanist failed to show up. Krips, aged eighteen, stepped in as substitute, accompanying some forty singers. To Weingartner's amazement, during the entire afternoon, Krips never referred to a piece of printed music. This incredible feat of memory convinced Weingartner that Krips was no ordinary orchestra musician. He engaged Krips at once as choirmaster, coach, and assistant conductor at the Volksoper. There, on September 3, 1921, Krips made his conducting debut in a performance of Verdi's opera, *The Masked Ball*. Three months after that, Krips directed his first symphony concert—at the Redoutensaal in Vienna. From then on, he divided his conducting energies and interests between opera and symphony.

Serving as principal conductor of opera in Aussig, Czechoslovakia, in 1924–25, and in Dortmund, Germany in 1925–26 was Krips's preparation for his first major assignment. This came in the fall of 1926 when he became general music director in Karlsruhe, one of the youngest men in Germany ever to fill such an important musical post. Here he was in full charge of all operatic and symphonic performances. In addition to his basic assignments he also led a special Bruckner festival in 1929 and a Handel festival in 1930 that attracted musical pilgrims from all over Germany. All this helped to establish his reputation, which was further enhanced during this year with successful guest spots with orchestras and opera companies throughout Germany and Austria.

After several fruitful years in Karlsruhe, Krips was appointed first conductor of the Vienna State Opera. His remarkable versatility in a wide range of Italian, French, and German operas attracted a good deal of admiration. His performances of Mozart and Wagner were on the level—so insisted many musical diehards in Vienna—with those formerly heard at the Vienna State Opera when Gustav Mahler and Bruno Walter conducted. Through his achievements not only at the State Opera but also at the Salzburg Festival (with which he first became associated in the summer of 1935), Krips became one of Austria's most highly venerated conductors.

But a political hurricane was sweeping across Europe. The Nazis had seized power in Germany, and in 1938 Nazi troops marched into Austria. As one of the most celebrated conductors in Europe, Krips seemed safe from the so-called "cleansing process" to which Nazis subjected German and Austrian music in ridding it of "undesirable" political and racial elements. But in their exhaustive researches into the backgrounds of all Austrian citizens, however highly placed, the Nazis discovered that a number of generations ago one of the Kripses had married a Jew. This immediately made Krips himself *persona non grata* in the new order in Austria.

For a short while, Krips tried to rehabilitate his shattered musical fortunes in Belgrade, Yugoslavia, where he conducted at the Opera and at the Philharmonic concerts. But Nazi influences were soon gaining an upper hand in Yugoslavia, too. Krips lost his jobs and had to return to Vienna. There, for the next eight years, he was forbidden to participate in any musical performances whatsoever. To earn his living he worked as a day laborer in a food-processing factory.

When the war ended, musical Vienna was in a shambles. Krips was drawn out of his long retirement and musical inactivity to help revive this dormant musical society. He set to work with a will, gathering all the singers and musicians he could find, and putting them through the paces of grueling rehearsals. He had to walk each day two hours from his home to the rehearsal and back, no other mode of transportation being available to him at the time. And at the rehearsal he had to spark half-starved and miserably paid singers and musicians into giving him the best they could. Finally, Mozart's *The Marriage of Figaro* was made ready to reopen the Volksoper—the first opera performance heard in Vienna in several years. That accomplishment behind him, Krips now devoted himself to the business of rebuilding the artistic forces of the Vienna State Opera and the Vienna Philharmonic. As the principal conductor of both of these historic organizations, he was able to restore to Vienna some of the glorious music-making which had been traditional with that city. By 1947, both the opera company and the orchestra were sufficiently restored to their one-time greatness to begin the first of three annual tours throughout Europe under Krips's direction.

In 1949, Krips was made first conductor of the London Symphony Orchestra. He held this assignment for six years while continuing to conduct at least a part of each year in Vienna. Meanwhile, in 1950, he was invited for the first time to the United States, being offered a number of guest appearances with the Chicago Orchestra at Ravinia Park. Upon arriving in New York he was detained by immigration officials on "political grounds" and refused admission into the United States before he could be cleared in an extensive hearing. Since Krips had never involved himself in any political activity, this matter upset him no end. Rather than submit to intensive grilling, he turned around and went back to Europe without giving his concerts. The reason why Krips was held under suspicion was never explained, but it was generally believed that a number of highly successful concerts he had given in the Soviet Union had made him suspect; and, it must be remembered, that in 1950 there did not yet exist a cultural exchange between the United States and the Soviet Union.

But in 1953 no obstacles were put in Krips's way to return to the United States, for by then a quiet and comprehensive investigation had proved to the immigration officials that there was nothing questionable about Krips's political leanings. He scored such a sensational success in his American debut as symphony conductor—with the Buffalo Philharmonic, on February 15, 1953—that he was invited the following year to take over the orchestra on a permanent basis. How highly the city of Buffalo came to regard their Maestro was proved in 1957 when he was named by the *Evening News* "citizen of the year" and was awarded the Chancellor's Medal by the University of Buffalo.

From then on, Krips divided his musical activities between the United States and Europe. In America he made guest appearances with major orchestras besides guiding the destinies of the Buffalo Philharmonic. In Europe and the Near East he was also a highly favored guest conductor. A Beethoven festival he conducted in Israel was one of the great cultural achievements of that little country. After a magnificent presentation of Bruckner's Eighth Symphony in Berne, Switzerland, he was awarded the Bruckner Medal of the Bruckner Society. And in 1962, in recognition of his outstanding artistic contributions to the city of Vienna, he was given one of its highest honors, the so-called *"Ehrenring,"* or "Ring of Honor."

During the 1962–63 season, Joseph Krips was named conductor and musical director of the San Francisco Symphony, but his tenure did not begin until the following season, with a gala performance on November 29, 1963. At the end of that concert he was accorded a fifteen-minute standing ovation. One local critic commented the next morning that "the golden age of music" had come to San Francisco. But whether in San Francisco or New York, Vienna or Salzburg, Paris or Tel Aviv, the golden age of music is always at hand when Krips is there to conduct the literature he loves best—the operas of Mozart and Wagner, and the symphonies of Beethoven, Brahms, and Bruckner.

HERBERT VON KARAJAN

[Born 1908]

SINCE THE END of World War II, Herbert von Karajan has been a musical Colossus bestriding virtually all of Europe. Few conductors have had a hand in so many musical pies at the same time as Karajan. Few have been, through the years, affiliated with so many significant European musical organizations. In 1948, he was made the artistic director of the Gesellschaft der Musikfreunde in Vienna where his symphony concerts soon came to be known as "Von Karajan cycles." In 1955 he was given a lifetime appointment as musical director of the Berlin Philharmonic in succession to Wilhelm Furtwaengler; this, one of Europe's most highly esteemed music posts, has since remained Karajan's home base from which he proceeds in all directions in Europe for his various musical operations. In 1956 he became the musical director of the Vienna State Opera, and in 1957 the artistic director of the world-famous Salzburg Festival in Austria, holding both assignments with remarkable success for about a decade, while still fulfilling his obligations to the Berlin Philharmonic. He was the director of the International Bach Festival in Vienna in 1950, and the conductor of the complete Wagner *Ring* cycle at the Bayreuth Festival. He has also been one of the principal conductors of the La Scala, Milan, Italy's most famous opera house, and of the Philharmonia Orchestra, one of London's finest in the post-World War II era.

His extraordinary career, studded so richly with successes of the first magnitude and in so many different places, has few parallels in conducting history. Karajan has become in Europe something more than just an extraordinary and world-famous musician. He has become what the Europeans designate as a *"Kulturidol"* and which we Americans refer to as a "matinee idol." Newspapers and magazines in Europe never tire of reporting his comings and goings, of describing his extra-musical hobbies, and of photographing him. He is the material on which newspaper and magazine stories thrive. He is tall, graceful, aristocratically dignified in manner, and so strikingly handsome he could easily be taken for a stage or screen star. His lithe, disciplined body betrays the fact that he is a natural athlete. He is an enthusiastic and highly skillful mountain climber and one of Austria's best amateur skiers. He knows how to maneuver a yacht on the Mediterranean waters. He is also adept at piloting his private plane (which he laughingly calls the "Karajan Airlines") and in sending his Ferrari sports car at a breakneck speed across tortuous mountain roads. He is the first musician ever to distinguish himself in such a fashion as a sportsman. The way he learned to water ski is an indication of how easily he takes to sports that interest him. He was watching a water-skiing performance at a sea resort. He borrowed a pair of skis, experimented for a number of hours, and then flew with amazing ease and skill over the waters.

Thus Karajan, at all times a fashion plate, cuts a dashing figure not only on the conductor's platform but in the pleasure domes of the world, whether in the lovely lake or mountain regions of Austria and Switzerland where he loves to spend his winter holidays, or on the sunbaked shores of the Riviera, or in exotic Casablanca. And his wife is an additional ornament. She is Eliette, a former Dior model, one of Europe's most exquisitely gowned and strikingly attractive women. She is Karajan's third wife, whom he married in 1958.

"For the average man on the street in Central Europe," wrote H. C. Robbins Landon, "what really is fascinating about Karajan is that he is totally unlike an intellectual. . . . As such he attracts the adulation of people who ordinarily consider conductors balding intellectuals who (in Europe) frequent coffee-houses and have soft bellies. . . . All this sort of thing has inspired a curiosity about his everyday life comparable only to public interest in personages of Hollywood—or *pace* Europe—Cannes. Karajan himself is reported to have said, 'They seem to think my conducting is only an interruption of my hobbies.' "

But (make no mistake about it!) Karajan *is* a conductor, and one of the greatest of the twentieth century—his many extra-curricular activities notwithstanding. He has committed the basic symphonic and operatic literature to memory, possesses such a thorough and staggering knowledge of the repertory that he rarely consults the printed page. His knowledge of the instruments of the orchestra and the human voice is all-embracing. Since he is an autocrat, he knows how to command and to get obeyed, so that the musical forces under his command are always in full control. He has exceptional interpretative gifts in a varied literature that ranges from Johann Sebastian Bach to the ultra-moderns of the twentieth century. In music with particular dramatic interest—the Wagnerian music dramas, Mussorgsky's *Boris Godunov,* or Bach's *Passion According to St. Matthew*, for example—he is probably with few if any rivals.

Sure of himself and his musical powers, equally sure of the spell he casts on audiences, Karajan has not been afraid to dream big dreams and then try to bring them to fulfillment. One of the reasons he left the Vienna State Opera in a huff, where for about a decade he had been lord and master, was because he wanted to work out an international scheme whereby the Vienna State Opera, Milan's La Scala, and New York's Metropolitan Opera collaborated all their resources in the performances of operas under his direction which would be the last word in musical presentation, staging, and costuming. The Vienna State Opera preferred going its own way, as had been its practice for over half a century, and the project remained stillborn, at least for the time being.

Then, in 1965, Karajan announced still another venture, even more vast in concept, universal in scope. This project consisted of the production of Wagner's *Ring* cycle over a four-year period, each of the music dramas being presented a year at a time, until the four had been staged. The finest singers and musicians in the world would collaborate with the fullest resources of present-day staging techniques, and the art and skill of the foremost living costume and scenic designers. In short, no expense would be spared to make this the ultimate in Wagnerian presentations. Each of the four dramas would be produced first in Salzburg, Austria, during the Easter season, the first drama projected for 1967. The production would then be repeated the following fall at the Metropolitan Opera in New York. Each of the productions would be filmed for distribution in motion-picture theaters and probably over television, and each would be recorded in its entirety. These plans have been described as probably the most ambitious ever undertaken in serious music. And only a Karajan would have dared to conceive them.

Herbert von Karajan was born in Salzburg, Austria, on April 5, 1908, of Macedonian-Greek-Austrian ancestry. His father, a surgeon, was a devoted music lover who played the clarinet in a local orchestra. He could be calculated to encourage his son's tendencies in music, particularly when these tendencies revealed themselves so early and so forcefully. As a child of about three and a half Herbert von Karajan would hide under the piano while his older brother took lessons. Then, the lessons over, the infant would try to reproduce on the keyboard what he had heard. He started lessons of his own at about this time. By five, he was able to make a public appearance. "One of my earliest recollections," Karajan says, "was a burning love of music, which made me forget to eat or sleep. I had perfect pitch without even knowing it. Wrong intonation and weak rhythm were painful to me." Music study, with emphasis on the piano, was continued in depth at the Salzburg Mozarteum. "My conception of what could come out of a piano was so exaggerated that my last piano teacher said one day, 'Try to become a conductor, otherwise you will never be satisfied.' He is the man to whom I am most grateful in my career. He is the famous Mozart expert, Dr. Bernhard Paumgartner." Later on, Karajan attended the University of Vienna where he specialized in philosophy and music history. He also took courses in conducting at the Academy of Music. "When I started conducting I suffered considerably because there was little opportunity for pupils to conduct. In two years of studying, I conducted no more than thirty minutes. Consequently, some of us conducting students formed an ensemble among ourselves, and we used to perform, nearly every day, the opera to be given at the State Opera that evening. We borrowed singers from vocal classes, two pianos, some strings, and one member sang for the choir.

So, at least, we obtained knowledge of the opera. And after hearing it in the evening we used to discuss it."

At last, in 1927, Karajan conducted a public concert for the first time. This performance made such an impression on the manager of the Ulm Municipal Theatre that he engaged Karajan as first conductor of his opera company. Karajan made his debut in Ulm with Mozart's *The Marriage of Figaro.* "Work in Ulm," he remembers, "was enormously difficult. There were just twenty-two orchestra members and the vocalists were only beginners because we could not pay for experienced ones. The conductor was all in one: coach, chorus master, conductor. When I did not conduct, I used to operate the lighting machinery to get the knowledge of everything concerned with the production. In spite of the small size of the orchestra, we had a full repertory, even including operas like Richard Strauss's *Salome.* When we gave concerts we had to borrow musicians from all possible sources, sometimes from the local military band. I recall going around town on a bicycle every morning to the symphony hall to collect all the musicians. Although artistically perhaps of limited value, my whole time in Ulm was important to me in subsequent years for I learned working from the bottom up."

After seven years in Ulm, Karajan went on to Aachen where, as music director, he was put in full charge of opera and symphony. Aachen had a fine orchestra, and one of the best choirs in Germany. "With the ensemble we used to give concerts in Holland and Belgium, and as I had to conduct about forty different symphonic programs a year, I acquired an extensive repertory." While employed at Aachen, Karajan gave guest performances in various European capitals, his reputation penetrating beyond the borders of Germany for the first time. In 1936 he made his first appearance at the Vienna State Opera in Wagner's *Tristan and Isolde,* a performance which was still remembered and admired many years later. In 1938 his international reputation increased when he gave successful performances at La Scala, Milan, at the Florence May Music Festival, and with the Berlin Philharmonic. Such was his triumph in Berlin that forthwith he was invited to be a guest conductor of the Berlin State Opera. One year after that he was given the conductorship of the Berlin State Opera Orchestra which presented regular series of symphony concerts. "It was a wonderful job with this fine orchestra and difficult only because I had to divide my time between Aachen and Berlin. Three or four times a week after a performance in Berlin I had to leave on a night plane, without even having time to change my clothes. Sometimes I had to fly there and back for a single rehearsal. By the end of three years it had become so trying that I had to resign my post in Aachen." In Berlin he came to be known as *"das wunder Karajan"* ("the Karajan miracle"), a phrase coined by a journalist for the *Berliner Zeitung.* He conducted the Wagnerian music dramas, as well as all his symphony concerts, from memory; and he led Bach's *Brandenburg Concertos* the way the old Kapellmeisters used to do in the eighteenth century, from a place at the harpsichord where he played the *continuo.*

Having settled in Berlin in 1941, Karajan succeeded Wilhelm Furtwaengler as first conductor of the Opera without relinquishing the Opera Orchestra concerts. He became a pet of Nazi high society and government leaders, with whose political and social philosophy he had been in full agreement for a number of years. This was the reason why, when Germany was defeated and World War II in Europe ended, Karajan was regarded *persona non grata* by the occupying American forces and was not given official permission to continue his musical career. He returned to his native Salzburg to lead for a while a quiet, secluded existence.

He first emerged from this retirement when Walter Legge, artistic director of the English recording company, the Columbia Gramophone, wrangled permission from the United States authorities to permit Karajan to make a number of recordings with the Vienna Philharmonic. This was the first step in Karajan's "denazification." The next one allowed him to give a number of concerts. Finally Karajan resumed a more active role as conductor by becoming the musical director of the Vienna Symphony, a not particularly distinguished ensemble when he took it over but which he fashioned into a major musical organization. He went on from there to lead the Vienna Philharmonic, to assume the direction of the Vienna Gesellschaft der Musikfreunde, to appear at the festivals at Salzburg, Florence, and Bayreuth, and to become the musical director of the-then newly founded Philharmonia Orchestra in London with which he toured Eruope. He was also affiliated with La Scala, where he was given full responsibilities for every phase of the production besides the musical ones, and with the Radio Italian Orchestra in Rome which was almost exclusively a broadcasting organization. He served as principal conductor of the Berlin Philharmonic during the city's cultural festival in 1954.

This period found him making a historic recording of Bach's B minor Mass with the combined forces of the Gesellschaft der Musikfreunde chorus and the Vienna Symphony; this was in 1951. He demanded and got seventy rehearsals before he was satisfied with the results and was ready to begin the first recording session. Two days before they were to begin, Karajan was stricken with blood poisoning. He had to conduct for the recording from a stretcher, unable to do much more than feebly raise one arm. "Nevertheless," he says, "the rapport among all the participants was so strong that the recording proved to be most outstanding."

While Wilhelm Furtwaengler lived, a bitter rivalry developed between him and Karajan for the top position in German music, which Furtwaengler had previously occupied alone for so many years. Each conductor had his own passionate followers who insisted that his man was the greater of the two. Then Furtwaengler died in 1954, and Karajan inherited Furtwaengler's post with the Berlin Philharmonic. From then on, Karajan's supremacy among conductors in Germany and Austria was uncontested.

A number of years ago, Karajan would go into a kind of trance before beginning to conduct a composition. He would stand motionless, his hands hanging limply at his side, while the silence in the auditorium became almost excrutiating. Then his arms would rise slowly, he would give the downbeat, and the performance would begin. But his trance remained unbroken. As he directed the music his eyes were closed and his face became transfigured by a kind of religious exaltation. "Part of this 'routine' was undoubtedly real," C. Robbins Landon explains, "and it must be stated . . . quite clearly: When he is making music Karajan is not in any sense a mountebank but a genuinely dedicated man. Nowadays he has gotten away from that prayerful attitude; the hypnotic concentration he is famous for is manifested just as strongly, but in different ways—for example, when he lays down his baton in the second act of *Tristan* and conducts with quiet, circular motions of his hands. Here the intensity is just as great and the theatricality of the closed-eyes stance has disappeared."

Karajan often told interviewers he holds no theories regard-
ing baton technique or a conductor's behavior on the podium.
"A baton, a pencil, it makes no difference. You tie my wrist to
my side and the orchestra will still get the beat. I tell my
pupils, 'You must feel the tempos and rhythms, and then the
orchestra will feel them.' "

Karajan's conducting is characterized primarily by intensity and strength. In dynamic passages with large sounds he
can be electrifying. But he also possesses an exquisite feeling
for the lyric line and a grace all his own in quiet and gentle
passages. He has a gift for making the strings sing, while the
rich and sonorous sounds he produces from the entire orchestra have a quality and texture all their own. "It took me
twelve years to get the kind of sound I want," he has said. He
now manages to draw that sound from whatever organization
he directs, to get it in a highly varied and extensive repertory.

In 1954, the Berlin Philharmonic was scheduled to make its
first tour of the United States, under its renowned music director, Wilhelm Furtwaengler. Furtwaengler died suddenly
before the tour began; the job fell into Karajan's hands. Consequently, the American debut of the Berlin Philharmonic,
and that of Karajan, took place simultaneously—late in February 1955 in Washington, D.C. When, a few days later, conductor and orchestra appeared in Carnegie Hall, New York,
Howard Taubman said in *The New York Times*: "Mr.
Karajan is a conductor of stature. Playing, Haydn, Wagner,
and Beethoven music, Mr. Karajan conducted . . . from
memory with very little fuss or furbelows, with a craftsman's
knowledge of this business and with an artist's understanding
of the music at hand. . . . He may be the best conductor in
Europe as his admirers claim for him. For the moment let it be
said here that he is a remarkably gifted one."

In the fall of 1955, Karajan toured the United States again, this time as the head of London's Philharmonia Orchestra. These were Taubman's second thoughts about him: "He proved that he is a conductor of major quality . . . a virtuoso leader. . . . The orchestra was utterly responsive to his musical requirements. . . . In the Mozart *Divertimento* . . . there were delicacy of tone, sensitivity of nuance, a feeling for the inner life of Mozart's thought. This was Mozart playing of the highest order. In *La Mer* there was . . . the utter sense of control by the conductor over all his instrumental resources. The design of Debussy's score was clear from beginning to end and the play of color was a thing of beauty. The *Fantastic Symphony* got a performance in which every last strand was in place. This was a virtuoso performance that few orchestras could equal."

In 1956, Karajan became the artistic director of the Vienna State Opera and principal conductor of the Vienna Philharmonic. For almost a decade he was the darling of Vienna's music lovers. But since he was an autocrat who tolerated no interference with his purpose and direction, friction often developed between himself and the powers who led the destinies of both these organizations. Finally Karajan felt he had to leave Vienna.

They tell a story about one of Karajan's rehearsals in Vienna which was being disturbed by the chirping of a bird, which had found a home in an airshaft. Every attempt to dislodge it proved of no avail. The bird continued to stay in its new found home, continued to sing whenever the orchestra started to play. Karajan remarked: "After all, he is a Viennese bird, and a musical bird and he cannot live without making music in Vienna."

There are many authorities who insist that Karajan is like

the bird in this anecdote. In spite of his many, varied and ambitious conducting assignments all over the face of Europe, he cannot long live without making Viennese music, since Vienna was the scene of his first major successes, and Vienna has a place all its own in Karajan's heart. But one thing is certain, as this writer had more than one opportunity to discover during the Vienna Festival Weeks in 1965. The Viennese people sorely miss not only Karajan's kind of music making but also his personal magnetism and striking physical appeal. The Viennese insist that Karajan some day will come back. Meanwhile, Karajan will continue to be one of the most important musicians in Europe.

OTTO KLEMPERER

[Born 1885]

In a review of Otto Klemperer's recording of Mozart's last symphonies, Nathan Broder said in *High Fidelity* magazine, in July 1965: "At the age of eighty, Otto Klemperer shows no sign of fatigue or diminution of enthusiasm. If anything, his performances grow even more polished, as well as more self-effacing, more completely at the service of the composer's thought. . . . At best he can reach the stars. . . . He is seldom far below that level."

An English reviewer, Deryck Cooke, was even more excited about still another Klemperer recording, this time of Beethoven's Ninth Symphony. He said: "Listening to this disc has been one of the great experiences of my life. . . . This is not only a disc of the month but a great recording of the century, indeed, the great recording of the century for me."

Appraisals like these for a conductor past his eightieth birthday are remarkable enough. Nevertheless, there have been conductors other then Klemperer who have soared to heights in old age—Pierre Monteux, Arturo Toscanini, Leopold Stokowski, to mention just three. What sets Klemperer apart from other octogenarian conductors—in fact what has made his career without a single parallel in all music, if not in all art—is the fact that he has reached the apex of his achievements in old age after destiny struck him not one but several devastating blows, each of which would have crushed any other man. Just to have survived from this succession of disasters, just to have been able to continue functioning, would have represented a monumental accomplishment. To be able to rise from such catastrophes to new and greater peaks of achievement is surely a tale of personal heroism, of artistic courage, and of the will to survive with few equals.

But let us start at the beginning of this dramatic biography.

Otto Klemperer was born in Breslau, Germany, on May 14, 1885. He was the grandson of a religion teacher, and the son of a merchant. When he was four, his family moved to Hamburg where the boy attended elementary school and started studying the piano with his mother. By the time he was sixteen he knew that his life's work would be music. He enrolled in Hoch's famous Conservatory in Frankfort-on-the-Main, then completed his musical training at the Klindworth-Scharwenka Conservatory in Berlin where his teachers included Hans Pfitzner in composition and James Kwast in piano.

Though trained to become a virtuoso pianist—and though for a year following his graduation from the conservatory he made the rounds of the concert stages in Germany—Klemperer early came to the conviction that he wanted to be a conductor. In 1905 he served a baton apprenticeship in Berlin as assistant to Oskar Fried. One year later, Max Reinhardt, Germany's distinguished stage director, picked Klemperer to conduct the music for his production of Offenbach's operetta, *Orpheus in the Underworld*. During this period Klemperer also found an opportunity to assist at a performance of one of

Gustav Mahler's symphonies. Mahler was already one of the most celebrated conductors of his generation (having created an epoch of unparalleled splendor at the Vienna Royal Opera), and he was also one of the most distinguished composers of his time. In the preparation of this performance Klemperer was often thrown into personal contact with this idealistic and inspiring conductor-composer. This proved a momentous experience for young Klemperer—an experience and a turning point. For Klemperer, Mahler now became a model for emulation, a source of inspiration. For his part, Mahler would, in the few years of life still left him, do what he could to promote young Klemperer's career. "I find Herr Klemperer extraordinarily good," Mahler wrote to the German Theater in Prague in recommending him for a conducting job. "I guarantee good results in case of his appointment to the post of conductor and always stand ready personally to cooperate with him and help him."

Such a recommendation could hardly be ignored. This letter brought Klemperer to Prague and to his first conducting assignment. He did so well there that in 1910 he was called to the Hamburg Opera as principal conductor, staying four years. Then he became the musical director of the Strassburg Opera and from 1917 to 1924 to the Cologne Opera. Two significant developments in Klemperer's life took place at Cologne. He conducted symphonic music for the first time. From this time on he would divide his energies and gifts between operas and orchestral music. And, also in Cologne, he got married. The girl was a soprano named Johanna Gaissler, who had appeared as soloist at one of his concerts. They were married in 1917.

From 1924 to 1927 Klemperer was musical director of the Wiesebaden Opera where his performances (especially of the moderns) attracted world interest. From 1927 until its dissolution in 1931, he headed the musical forces of the Kroll Opera in Berlin. At these two opera theaters, as well as in his performances with major German symphony orchestras, Klemperer proved himself one of the giants among European conductors. He had a fabulous memory, a commanding personality, an extraordinary musicianship, a formidable self-discipline. He was also a highly controversial musician. He was always involved in wrangles with singers, scenic designers, directors, and orchestra men because he refused to accept anything but the highest possible standards. He became the object for severe criticism because he was such a passionate advocate of modern music. But beyond these considerations he often alienated even some of those who had been impressed by his musical capabilities because of his gruff manner, hot tempers, brusque attitudes, despotism, and garrulousness. Yet, in spite of the fact that he aroused passions all around him, he also inspired admiration. Time and again he was the recipient of high public honors as when President Paul von Hindenburg of Germany presented him with the Goethe medal for "outstanding contribution to German culture."

Klemperer was beginning to make important appearances outside Germany, notably in England and Russia. Then, on January 24, 1926, he made his bow in the United States when he appeared as a guest of the New York Symphony Society. This writer, who attended that debut, remembers that performance vividly because of its striking individuality. Klemperer led a program made up of three symphonies, one each by Haydn, Mozart, and Beethoven, all of which he both rehearsed and performed from memory. He was such a towering figure on the stage—standing six feet, six—that he did not need a platform to elevate him above the musicians. As he conducted, he crouched, stooped, swayed. At times, when he threw his arms in a broad arc, he resembled an eagle ready to swoop down on its prey. His musicianship and his knowledge of the scores could not be questioned, nor, for that matter, his ability to control the orchestra. But to this writer he appeared that day a diamond in the rough. He could not always keep in check the dynamic and emotional forces he released. He had power and strength in his interpretations; but he lacked sensitivity. His readings had scabrous edges. He overemphasized the significance of the double basses, brasses, and timpani. He was partial to excessive rubatos; he often disregarded fermatas; and he sometimes permitted loud or fast passages to get out of hand. There were many moments in Beethoven's Seventh Symphony, and especially in the finale, when such an approach and such methods served the music well; and at these times Klemperer was one of the most exciting conductors in the world. We knew then that he had the makings of greatness, but whether he would ever fully realize that greatness through discipline, sobriety, and sensitivity was a question that could not be answered in 1925.

Both the audiences and the critics were divided in their reactions to that Klemperer performance. As for the men in the orchestra, they disliked him intensely, and made no effort to conceal their antagonism. For one thing, many of the musicians in the New York Symphony were either French or Italian. All of them were still violently prejudiced against Germans, since the memory of World War I was then still fresh in heart and mind. Then, it must be confessed, Klemperer did not help to appease their anti-German feelings with tact, charm, or grace. At rehearsals he was tyrannical, condescending, smugly superior, and at times even contemptuous. To make matters still worse, he talked and talked and talked, making the explanations of what he wanted from the men into long, dull dissertations. One time, when one of his lectures appeared interminable, the first oboist, an Italian, interrupted him by shouting from across the stage: "Mr. Klemps, you talka too much!" Klemperer's peculiar and highly personal ideas of tempo often upset the soloists. A world famous pianist was rehearsing a Beethoven concerto with him when he shouted from the piano: "Mr. Klemperer, the conductor is *there*, but the soloist is *here!*", meaning that the conductor was just the accompanist and that the final decisions of interpretation rested with the soloist. Klemperer fixed his cold, severe stare on the performer and replied angrily: "The conductor is *here* and the soloist is *there*, but where, sir, is Beethoven?"

In those years, Klemperer needed the refinement and humility and self-effacement that stem from full artistic maturity. As it turned out in the end, these qualities *did* eventually make him one of the supreme conductors of the twentieth century. But even before this happened, he was gathering success after success. In 1927, for example, he was invited to the Soviet Union to direct a Beethoven festival commemorating the centenary of the master's birth; his performances in Moscow and Leningrad were triumphs.

The first of several shattering blows leveled at him by an unkindly fate took place in Leipzig, soon after Klemperer had come there in the early 1930s as head of its Opera. While rehearsing, he leaned back against a protective railing placed around him. It gave way and he fell backwards. As he toppled off the stage, he struck the base of his skull against the stage, suffering severe concussions. He was unconscious for hours, and for weeks he was desperately ill. He finally recovered, though never completely. From then on he was a chronic victim of severe headaches and occasional fainting spells. Nevertheless, he kept on conducting; and he kept on growing as an artist.

He had hardly the opportunity to recover from this tragic accident when another blow came his way. The year was now 1933. The Nazis were in power in Germany, and their basic policy was to rid the country of Jews. Although he held a high musical post, that of conductor at the Berlin State Opera where he had then been recently engaged, and though he was now one of Europe's most celebrated musicians, he became the target for attack by the Nazis. They forced him to resign his job. He was attacked not only in the press, but even physically in the streets by Storm Troopers. To save his life, Klemperer had to flee the country.

He came to the United States where he tried to rebuild a shattered career. In New York he led some concerts with the New York Philharmonic and a series of orchestral performances over the radio. In Pittsburgh, he helped to reorganize its orchestra. Most significantly, he was appointed musical director of the Los Angeles Philharmonic, retaining this post for six years between 1933 and 1939. Ever richer, ever deeper, ever more mature grew his interpretations as year after year he helped to make what had formerly been a provincial orchestra into a symphonic organization of outstanding artistic significance. He was able to build up that orchestra and to develop his own artistic sensibilities in spite of the fact that he was suffering physically all the time. His headaches grew worse. At the same time his moods were becoming increasingly irascible, his attitudes increasingly belligerent. Finally, in 1939, the physicians diagnosed his condition as a tumor on the brain. An operation followed from which Klemperer emerged with his right side paralyzed. "He lay there in a wheelchair, his eyes glassy, not focused on anything in the world," one unidentified journalist wrote in describing his impressions of Klemperer after that operation. "One side of his face was dead, so was his right hand. It hung there, still and lifeless, as if it knew it could never hold a baton again."

His career—if not his life—seemed at a dead end. This fact was made plain to the world at large and to Klemperer's closest friends. But it was a fact that Klemperer himself would not contemplate. He was determined to get well again, to conduct again. Grimly he set about the business of rehabilitating a shattered body, first by learning to use crutches, then by going through the most stringent exercises in his attempt to bring life back to his inert limbs. "Rarely had there been a more spectacular demonstration of will power's efficacy as medicine," said Peter Whitelam in *Hi-Fi Review*. "Physically he was still weak, and his mind was not yet adjusted to the new handicaps, but his indomitable urge to resume his career could not be denied."

When he felt he was ready to return to music he discovered that nobody was willing to take a chance on him. Managers insisted that he would never again be well enough in body and spirit to resume his professional career, and they refused to be partners to a devastating fiasco. But Klemperer closed his eyes to defeat. Depleting his life's savings, he hired a seventy-five piece orchestra and gave a concert in Carnegie Hall in an exacting program that included works by Bach and Mozart, Beethoven's *Eroica* Symphony and Hindemith's *Noblissima Visione*. Klemperer was fighting for his artistic life, just as a number of months back he had been fighting for his physical life. In this battle he gave what some in the audience felt was one of the most exalted performances of his entire career.

But fate was still stacking the cards against Klemperer. Europe was soon at war. Engagements there, of course, were non-existent. In America, to which so many foreign conductors had come in search of jobs, the scramble for conducting assignments was too keen and spirited for Klemperer to compete successfully in view of his physical history. He was forced into retirement.

He bided his time. With the war over, he started his career all over again, sometimes by making recordings, sometimes by making random appearances in Italy, France, and Germany. In spite of physical weariness, in spite of old age, his playing was untouched by either fatigue or despair. The audience and critics began to accept him again. An extensive tour was mapped out. Then, in October 1951, Klemperer fell down a flight of stairs at the airport in Montreal. His thigh was broken in two places. Confined again to a wheel chair, he had to cancel the projected tour. In fact he was told by his physicians in no uncertain terms that his musical life was now definitely over.

But the physicians had not counted on Klemperer's Herculean will. He left that wheelchair to undertake European tours, even though he had to struggle painfully toward the podium, supporting himself on two canes. He was even able for a time to assume the post of musical director of the Budapest Opera. He was infirm, he was old, he was even immobile, and he was always in pain. He had to conduct while seated in a chair. But once he took baton in hand he was young again in spirit, and in his full maturity as an artist.

One evening in Cologne, in 1955, while conducting Mozart's *Don Giovanni*, Klemperer was so deeply immersed in making music that at one point in the performance he forgot his infirmity completely. He rose from his seat and stood on his own feet for the first time in several years. The artistic and spiritual rehabilitation that had been taking place with him had now become physical as well.

And in the performances he has given since 1955 all over Europe, and in his prodigious recordings, he appeared as an altogether *new* Klemperer. Here is how Peter Whitelam put it: "There were signs that Klemperer had at last achieved peace of mind. The courage and nobility of his character that informed his music making now stood revealed in a different light. Where stern discipline and relentless drive had been dominant before, there was now a feeling of Olympian order and tender compassion."

LORIN MAAZEL

[Born 1930]

O F ALL THE areas of musical activity, conducting is probably the one least receptive to child prodigies. There have been one or two children who, from time to time, have stepped in front of an orchestra, baton in hand, and led performances for which they had come equipped with an innate feeling for rhythm, a sensitive ear, and sophisticated musical intelligence. Sometimes these prodigy conductors made a good impression. But this has been such a truly rare achievement that one can count the number of such successful appearances during the past half century on the fingers of a single hand with one or two fingers to spare. Conducting makes such a demand on a musician's intelligence, culture, training, and experience that talent alone cannot serve; and a child can hardly bring to his performances more than talent. Lorin Maazel, who *should* know, is himself of the opinion that "a prodigy conductor is almost a contradiction in terms. The very definition of conducting implies the communication of a matured interpretative concept. In spite of what it says, a child shall *not* lead."

Child-prodigy conductors, then, have been few and far between. Scarcer still is the number of prodigies who have grown into mature and distinguished conductors. In fact, in the past half century only one has succeeded in doing so. He is Lorin Maazel. Today Maazel is second only to Herbert von Karajan as Germany's favorite man with the baton—young though he still is. For a decade already Europe has come to regard him as one of the most exciting, one of the most inspiring men to be found on the podium.

The fact that Maazel started out as a prodigy and ended up as a great artist is only one of several ways in which he is in a class by himself. Another thing that sets Maazel apart from other American conductors is that he is the only one who received his adult experiences as conductor and achieved all his early major successes in Europe rather than America. There is still a third thing to make Maazel unique. He is the first American ever to be invited to conduct at the world-famous Wagnerian shrine, Bayreuth; he was also the youngest of *any* nationality to do so, being then only thirty. This happened during the summer of 1960 when he led eight performances of *Lohengrin*. What made this Bayreuth debut—and its attending success—even more remarkable and startling was that this was the first time that Maazel was conducting in an opera house.

Lorin Maazel was born in Paris on March 5, 1930. Both parents were Americans, and both were musicians who had come to Paris to continue their study of music. The Maazel family home was in Los Angeles, and it was there that the Maazels returned in 1932. This, of course, was a household in which music was always being played, sung, or talked about. Before long, the parents began to notice that their son Lorin was responding to music with concentration and rapt interest. He was just a child of four when they learned he had been born with absolute pitch; at five he demonstrated such a curiosity for the violin and such a determination to make music with it that he was given his first lessons. A few weeks after that he revealed he had been born not only with a sensitive ear but with a sponge-like memory. He had merely to play a piece through once and he remembered every note and marking on the page.

One day, when he was seven, he was found absorbed with a full orchestral score of Haydn's *Surprise Symphony*. When his mother asked him what he was doing he replied simply that he was "reading it from top to bottom." Then he proceeded to sing some of the principal themes. When the mother put on a recording of the symphony, the child started to wave his arms in rhythmical patterns. He had already attended a few symphony concerts and had seen conductors work; now, almost instinctively, he was trying to be a conductor himself.

He was placed with Vladimir Bakaleinikoff, a distinguished Los Angeles musician, who began teaching him the elements of conducting. So close a tie was established between teacher and pupil that when Bakaleinikoff moved to Pittsburgh in 1938 to become assistant conductor of its orchestra, the Maazels went with him so that Lorin's musical training might not be forced to take a different course. Bakaleinikoff remained Maazel's only formal teacher.

The following summer, Maazel attended the famous music camp at Interlochen, Michigan. It was there that he conducted an orchestra for the first time. This performance made such an impression on Olin Downes, the music critic of *The New York Times*, that he arranged for the boy to make an appearance at the New York World's Fair. There the nine-year-old boy made a formal concert debut by directing Mendelssohn's *Italian Symphony* and Tchaikovsky's *Marche*

Slave among other compositions. After the closing chords of the Tchaikovsky piece, reported Louis Biancolli in the New York *World-Telegram*, "the maestro toddled down . . . tugged at his shorts and ran towards the waiting arms of his mother and father. . . . You had to rub your eyes to believe it—this chubby little figure in a white linen suit pace-making for an orchestra of seventy, and giving every cue on the dot."

Arthur Judson, America's most influential concert manager, then and there signed Maazel to a contract. A performance at the Lewisohn Stadium in New York followed in the summer of 1940. This, in turn, led to a guest appearance with the NBC Symphony—at the personal invitation of Toscanini. Some of the musicians in that orchestra still remember Maazel's first rehearsal. He was dressed in breeches and open-collar white basque shirt, like a boy about to go out into the street and play with other children. He rapped the baton sharply on the stand for attention. His round, chubby face now became tense; his small eyes were shining; his child's brow creased in concentration. The musicians were at first amused at the picture the child presented on a podium hallowed by Toscanini. They entered into the rehearsal almost in a spirit of child's play. But they were soon taken aback when the child stopped them with the very first wrong note and made the necessary correction. Then, when the musicians were brought face to face with the realization that this child was not performing just a stunt but was equipped with the memory, ear, and instincts to give a creditable performance their supercilious smiles disappeared, and they began working with a will.

Maazel continued making guest appearances with major orchestras during the next few years, invariably first inspiring amused attention and interest, and then encouraging admiration and awe. And then the inevitable took place. The child grew into adolescence; Maazel was a prodigy no longer. Aged fifteen, he saw engagements melt away. "I had lost my market value as a monstrosity," is the way he explains this development.

Maazel had arrived at that point in his career where so many musical prodigies fall by the wayside. It was a sober period, a time for re-evaluating his career and making fresh designs for the future. Wisely, Maazel decided it was also a time for returning to schooling, academic as well as musical. He enrolled in the University of Pittsburgh where he specialized in languages and philosophy. At the same time he continued making music wherever and whenever he could: by making a concert debut as violinst when he was sixteen; by organizing and playing in the Fine Arts String Quartet; finally by becoming a member of the violin section of the Pittsburgh Symphony.

After three years Maazel decided it was time for him to resume his interrupted conducting career. In 1948 he was named assistant conductor of the Pittsburgh Symphony. He helped rehearse the orchestra, worked long and hard, and revealed in everything he said and did that he was a conductor to the manner born. Victor de Sabata, one of Italy's eminent conductors, who had come to Pittsburgh for guest appearances, told him: "You will be one of the great of your generation."

Several important things happened to Maazel in 1951. Serge Koussevitzky invited him to the Berkshire Music Festival at Tanglewood to lead a performance of Stravinsky's *Symphony of Psalms*. Whoever heard them that day knew at once that the one-time prodigy had ripened into mature musician. At Tanglewood, Maazel met Mimi Sandbank, an American girl of Brazilian background, who was studying the piano at the Berkshire Music Centre. They fell in love and got married in June 1952. Then a third major development for Maazel followed. He received a Fulbright scholarship for research in fifteenth- and sixteenth-century music. This allowed him to return to Europe in 1952, which he made his home for the next decade. There he absorbed himself with research in baroque music, but at the same time he was waiting for some opportunity to prove himself again as conductor.

As so often happens in the lives of conductors, Maazel found that opportunity when a scheduled conductor was unable to fill his engagement. This happened in Catania, Sicily. Maazel, then living in Milan, was telephoned to take on the concert. He missed the scheduled train, sat up all night on another, and finally arrived at Catania too late for rehearsals. Nevertheless, he made an appearance—on Christmas Eve of 1953—and the performance went smoothly; but it attracted little attention outside of Sicily.

It was six months before Maazel got another chance to conduct. This time he gave a radio concert over an Italian network. Several Italian impresarios heard him and found guest spots for him with several orchestras. By 1956, Maazel was beginning to appear throughout all of Italy; by 1957, he was being heard all over Europe. Successes were mounting so rapidly that in 1957 he was chosen to open the Vienna Festival, and in 1958 he was invited to do a similar service for the Edinburgh Festival where he was heard in a monumental performance of Beethoven's *Missa Solemnis*. By 1959 he was one of Europe's prime conducting favorites, so much so that Bayreuth engaged him to conduct *Lohengrin* at its 1960 festival in spite of his youth, in spite of the fact that he was an American and, most unbelievably, in spite of the fact that up to now he had never conducted in an opera house. By 1960 he was conducting an average of fifty concerts a year and was getting the highest fee of any European conductor with the exception of Herbert von Karajan.

What impressed Europe was Maazel's command of symphonic literature which one critic described as "awesome"; his fiery personality that made his performances glow like hot coals; and his sure baton technique. Paul Moor wrote: "Since he has the score in his head, he can devote his eyes entirely to the musicians, and he shoots his glances everywhere . . . in advance of every important entrance or tricky passage, while the baton in his right hand gives a surgically exact beat and his left hand flashes signals of balance and dynamics. . . . Every movement has its motivation, and although he cuts a slimly elegant figure on the podium, his motions never become corybantic. . . . Aside from his musical mastery, his domination of the orchestra is a matter of sheer will and forcefulness of personality, which radiate from him both on and off the podium in an almost visible aura.

He had, consequently, soared to the top of his profession in Europe before getting heard again in America. He made his return as a mature, fully realized artist on October 1, 1962, at Philharmonic Hall in New York when he appeared as the conductor of the visiting L'Orchestre National Français. In a program comprising four symphonic standbys of past and present, Maazel conducted, as Harold C. Schonberg reported in *The New York Times,* "soberly and clearly, with plenty of strength and rhythm and a thorough feeling for . . . musical organization. . . . Mr. Maazel demonstrated that he had complete control over his orchestra, that he knew every note in the scores (he cues with head and shoulders as well as both hands) and that he is a musician with the technique and

146

knowledge to put his ideas into effect without any question."

Exactly one month after that, Maazel made his American debut as an opera conductor at the Metropolitan Opera in Mozart's *Don Giovanni*, which he led from memory. "There was a thorough understanding of the mood of the opera," Schonberg now said. "Its bigness, its underlying terror were not lost. . . . It was strong, logical conducting, superbly in balance and individual in concept."

And so, Maazel became the first American conductor to become a hero in the United States only after he had triumphed in Europe. "That he will become a hero," Schonberg added, "is as certain as C. P. Snow's Second Law. He has everything on his side."

Despite these and subsequent successes in the United States, Maazel established himself firmly and permanently in Europe when, in 1965, he became the musical director of the West Berlin Opera and permanent conductor of Berlin's Radio Symphony Orchestra (which is the city's most important orchestra next to the Philharmonic). The three-year agreement takes up seven months of Maazel's year. The rest of the time he makes guest appearances with symphony orchestras and opera companies the world over. He enjoys a few quiet weeks of vacation at his beautiful villa on Italy's Mediterranean coast with his wife and daughter. The Maazels also have an apartment in Rome on the top floor of a place in the center of the city near the Tiber River (where Benito Mussolini had lived in 1922).

Escape from the pressures of music making and music study comes to Maazel by going to a movie, or working out problems in or reading texts on mathematics. As a boy Lorin Maazel used to be interested in sports—mainly swimming, boating, horseback riding, and bicycling. Today he prefers diversions which tax the mind rather then the muscles of the body: memorizing liberettos of operas he plans to conduct, for example. He speaks half a dozen languages fluently. This fact became general knowledge a number of years ago when he made a recording of Benjamin Britten's *The Young Person's Guide to the Orchestra*. This score has a spoken part for narrator which Maazel himself performed in English, French, Italian, Spanish, Portuguese, and German, in different recordings for distribution in the various countries.

ZUBIN MEHTA

[Born 1936]

Not since the 1940s, when Leonard Bernstein's fame illuminated the musical horizons like a flaming meteor, has there appeared in the United States a young conductor to capture the imagination and enthusiasm of audience and critics the way Zubin Mehta has done. The fact that he comes from the East—the first Indian to achieve international recognition in music—has, of course, helped to glamorize him, to make him choice copy. But Mehta's amazing career would have been impossible if he had not come fully equipped for success, with one of the most fantastic intellects and one of the most electrifying personalities in music today. From the moment he appears on the stage, his head bent slightly, his pace measured—appearing like a Brahmin priest come to perform a religious ritual—the atmosphere in the concert hall or opera house becomes charged. His broad, sweeping gestures seem always to be in rigid control in spite of the wide arcs; those gestures are there, one is always convinced, not for visual display but to guide, instruct, and arouse the musicians in their performances. As the music progresses, the musicians feel that his eyes acquire a kind of hypnotic intensity, and burn like flame, while his face glows as though an inner light has been turned on. He has a sure theatrical instinct as well as a musical one. Says William Malloch: "He has an inborn sense of drama which he communicates to orchestra and audience. Instantaneously the music flashes; everything flashes." Or as Harriet Johnson, the music critic of the *New York Post*, once put it: "He has a spectacular gift that unites the mystery of the East with everything the West calls a great talent. . . . The curve of the phrase flows effortlessly into a mounting drama of lesser or greater suspense. His music emerges intensely from the shape of the music and in the Buddhist tradition is as strong in quiet as in action."

In *The New Yorker*, Winthrop Sargeant called Mehta "a remarkable master of the art of conducting." He adds: "His gestures . . . bespeak an ease in the conductor's role and a deep knowledge of the function of the baton that one would ordinarily attribute to long experience. His sense of rhythm is phenomenal. . . . He is also extremely sensitive to the shifting dynamics, the phrasing, the over-all form of a composition. Beyond this, he has a special feeling for poise, repose, and majesty, such as it is not often found among conductors of his generation. . . . He is an artist of extraordinary gifts."

Mehta, then, has the musicianship, personality, will, dramatic instincts, glamour and the gift to generate excitement through his very presence on the stage, which every conductor must possess in order to achieve the ultimate heights. With Mehta these qualities revealed themselves early, and for this reason his success came early. He became the youngest man ever to become the permanent conductor of a major American symphonic organization when, at twenty-six, he was appointed to the Los Angeles Philharmonic. He is the only conductor who, before he reached thirty, had directed the renowned Vienna Philharmonic and Berlin Philharmonic; had toured the Soviet Union, which he had done so successfully in 1962 with the Montreal Symphony; had appeared at the world-famous Salzburg Festival, where his performance of Mozart's *The Abduction from the Seraglio* in 1965 became one of the shining artistic events that summer. Before his thirtieth birthday he was acclaimed in most of the other leading European music festivals, including those at Lucerne, Montreux, Zurich, Cologne, and Prague. Still under thirty he made a momentous debut at the Metropolitan Opera in Verdi's *Aida* on December 29, 1965, and with the Philadelphia Orchestra a month before. Only two months after his thirtieth birthday he was invited to direct at Wagner's festival at Bayreuth.

Adding further to an illustrious, possibly unique, career before the age of thirty, is the fact that he became the only conductor ever to serve as music director of two major North American orchestras simultaneously (the Los Angeles Philharmonic and the Montreal Symphony); to participate in the dedication of three new major concert halls, which he did within the space of three months in 1964–65 (the Pavilion of the Music Center in Los Angeles, La Place des Arts in Montreal, and the New Civic Theatre in San Diego). No wonder, then, that *Time* has said that Mehta has "enjoyed one of the most spectacular ascents to fame in many a decade," and that Mehta's teacher in conducting, Hans Swarowsky, insists that Mehta will soon become "*the* dominant musical force in America and Europe."

One of the reasons why Mehta achieved success so soon in so many places was because all he needed was a single performance to prove himself. His first triumphs came after he had appeared in pinch-hitting roles. A conductor fell ill in Yugoslavia two days before concert-time. Eugene Ormandy was unable to fill a date with the Vienna Philharmonic in Vienna. Fritz Reiner had to cancel his concerts in Los Angeles. In each of these instances, Zubin Mehta, not yet twenty-five, stepped into the batter's box and hit the ball squarely and far.

That pinch-hitting assignment in Los Angeles is of particular importance, since it was responsible for bringing him his permanent job there. He had to fly in from Vienna to substitute for Fritz Reiner, who had suddenly fallen ill. He arrived at the rehearsal dressed in a black jersey sweater and in black slacks. Without opening the score, he gave the downbeat for Richard Strauss's tone poem, *Don Quixote*. Throughout the rest of that rehearsal period he worked from memory, electrifying the men with his vast knowledge of the music and the clear conception he had of the way it should be given. That one rehearsal was enough to convince the musicians that *here* was a born conductor. From that time on, they were all his stanchest supporters. The season after that, Mehta was brought back to Los Angeles for additional guest appearances. In 1962–63, when Georg Solti resigned as permanent conductor of the Los Angeles Philharmonic, Mehta signed a three-year contract as his replacement.

Zubin Mehta was born in Bombay, India, on May 29, 1936. He is a Parsee, which means that he is descended from the ancient Persians who had fled to India during the sixth century after Mohmanned's followers overran the Middle East. "The main principles of our religion," Mehta says, "are based on the symbolic virtues: good thoughts, good deeds, good words. It is the first religion that clarified the principals of spiritual cleanliness."

The father, Mehli Mehta, was the conductor of the Bombay Orchestra. Music, therefore, attended Zubin from his earliest childhood. "From the cradle on I heard chamber music," Zubin Mehta recalls. "I got acquainted with the Beethoven quartets before I ever heard a symphony. I could sing all this music before I could read a note."

Nevertheless, once he came into contact with orchestral music, he knew that he had found his first love in music. With his fantastic memory and fabulous ear he could assimilate the literature of symphonic music at first contact. While still in his boyhood, he helped out his father in rehearsing the Bombay Orchestra; on one or two occasions he substituted for his father at the concert. "I always had the intention of becoming a conductor," he says, "not just because I wanted to wave a stick, but because orchestral music appeals to me most. Otherwise I would have played the piano."

He was sent to Vienna to complete his music study at the Academy of Music. There he specialized in double bass performance, piano, and composition. "I went through the mill. At one time I had to take twelve courses at once. When he was graduated from the Academy, however, it was with a diploma in conducting, having studied the subject intensively with Hans Swarowsky, once a close associate of Richard Strauss. Mehta was twenty-one. His formal musical education was over. He stood ready to embark on a professional career.

In 1958, the Liverpool Philharmonic in England held a competition for young conductors. A hundred entered the contest. Mehta won first prize which entitled him to a job as the orchestra's assistant conductor for a season.

His career unfolded resplendently after that—and swiftly. His American debut took place during the summer of 1961 when he conducted the orchestra at the Lewisohn Stadium in New York. Less than two years after that he was the musical director not of one but two major symphony orchestras—the

Los Angeles Philharmonic and the Montreal Symphony. Meanwhile he had been heard and honored in Yugoslavia, Vienna, Berlin, Israel, and the Soviet Union. As *Variety* made note late in 1965: "He has covered more career ground in the five years since his obscure debut at the Lewisohn Stadium concert than any conductor around." At the same time he left little doubt that his journey to greatness has only just begun.

INDEX

155

INDEX

156

ABOUT THE AUTHOR

David Ewen has written over forty books on every facet of music—serious and popular—for adults and for young people. *Time* Magazine described him as "music's interpreter to the American people," and his books have been translated into over a dozen foreign languages.

Mr. Ewen published his first book in 1931, and since then not a year has passed without at least one of his titles appearing on a publisher's list. In the field of serious music his most popular works include *Encyclopedia of the Opera, Encyclopedia of Concert Music, The Complete Book of 20th Century Music, The World of Great Composers, David Ewen Introduces Modern Music,* and *The New Book of Modern Composers.* He has written biographies of George Gershwin, Jerome Kern, and Richard Rogers. Among his books on popular music are *The Complete Book of the American Musical Theater, Panorama of American Popular Music,* and *The Life and Death of Tin Pan Alley.*

In 1962–1963, Mr. Ewen wrote and co-produced a series of fifty-two broadcasts tracing the history of American popular music, which was beamed all over the world, in two dozen languages and dialects, by the Voice of America. Mr. Ewen's books for young people include biographies of George Gershwin, Jerome Kern, Richard Rogers, Leonard Bernstein, Arturo Toscanini, Johann Strauss, Joseph Haydn, Irving Berlin, and Cole Porter, as well as *Famous Instrumentalists.*

Date Due

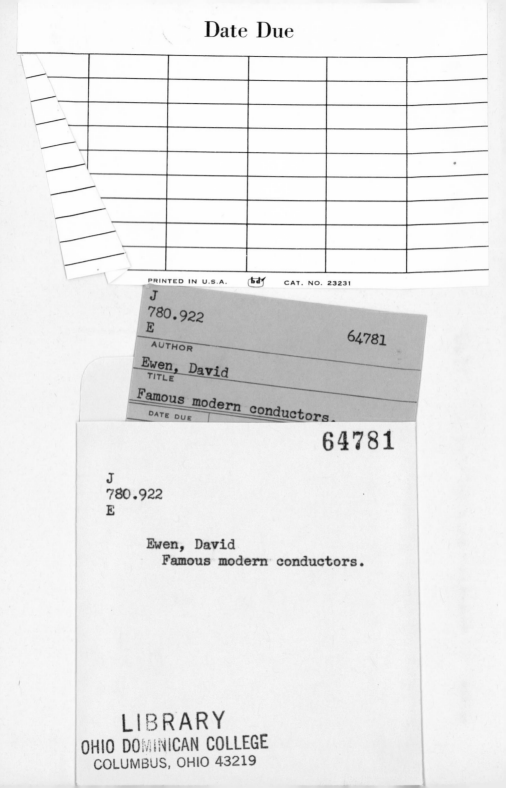